David
Dec-

W9-CNJ-699

REREADING LITERATURE
Ben Jonson

Ben Jonson

Peter Womack

Basil Blackwell

To Ray Ockenden

Copyright © Peter Womack 1986

First published 1986
First published in the USA 1987

Basil Blackwell Ltd
108 Cowley Road, Oxford OX4 1JF, UK

Basil Blackwell Inc.
432 Park Avenue South, Suite 1503,
New York, NY 10016, USA

British Library Cataloguing in Publication Data

Womack, Peter
    Ben Jonson. —— (Rereading literature)
    1. Jonson, Ben —— Criticism and interpretation
    I. Title II. Series
    822'.3   PR 2638

    ISBN 0-631-14375-0
    ISBN 0-631-14376-9 Pbk

Library of Congress Cataloging in Publication Data
Womack, Peter, 1952–
    Ben Jonson.
    (Rereading literature)
    Includes index.
    1. Jonson, Ben, 1573?–1637 — Criticism and
    interpretation. I. Title. II. Series.
    PR2638.W65 1986   822'.3   86-13698
    ISBN 0-631-14375-0
    ISBN 0-631-14376-9 (pbk.)

Typeset in Baskerville by Photo-graphics, Honiton, Devon
Printed in Great Britain by Whitstable Litho Ltd, Kent

Contents

Editor's Preface

Throughout Ben Jonson's work there runs a duality or contradiction which has helped to endear him to orthodox criticism. On the one hand he is admirably learned, judicious, authoritative and neo-classical, the very type of 'high' conservative humanist art; on the other hand he is engagingly earthy and boisterous, full of a robust 'English' vitality which disdains metaphysical pretension or frigid formalism. His patrician satire is no stranger to a certain populist, even anarchic impulse; if his malicious tongue lashes the mob, it also appears to speak their own patois as racily as themselves. The squire with a soft spot for the poacher has always been a cherished figure in English class mythology, and recent English political history has been deeply stamped by what some have termed authoritarian populism. The recurrent ideological fantasy of an aristocracy in close, sensuous touch with the people finds one of its cultural expressions in a suitably pliable, earth-bound English neo-classicism, tolerantly sceptical, in the manner of a Henry Fielding, of an absolutism about which it is nevertheless deadly serious.

Peter Womack's rereading of Jonson's drama seizes upon this contradiction and, through the mediation of the work of Mikhail Bakhtin, gives it a wholly different meaning. In an age of centralizing political absolutism, of which humanism's dream of a language purely transparent to truth is the obedient servant, Jonson's 'monological' urge to order, unify, separate and exclude is an instrument of political power. But this 'centripetal' impulse in Jonson's severely corrective poetics finds itself constantly outrun and undermined by a 'centrifugal', carnivalesque diversity, evident not least in the material, metonymic, monstrously proliferating nature of the Jonsonian word. In a brilliant move, Womack shows how theatre itself, with its creaking material mechanisms and bag of reach-me-down rhetorical devices, scandalously jeopardizes any pure, non-carnal communication between author and audience, interposing its ungainly bulk between stage signifier and textual signified to disseminate meanings beyond authorial control. The theatre of Jonson's time is just setting out on that historical path which will see the disappearance of the actor into the 'character' and of the audience into the darkness, repressing its own material nature in the name of what Womack calls a 'unified dramatic consciousness'. But if there is the 'absolutist' theatre of the courtly masque, whose point of unity is the singular figure of the monarch viewing it, there is also still for Jonson the public stage, whose socially mixed audience finds a reflection in the notable 'heteroglossia' or diversity of speech-modes within his own texts. Such social diversity is reflected too in the very figure of the Jacobean dramatist himself, who is both protégé of the powerful and petty bourgeois entrepreneur, dissident intellectual and part of an expanding capitalist enterprise.

In an age when the very concept of dramatic 'character' is gradually becoming a device to fix and stabilize the fluidity of social life, Jonson's stage figures remain, in Womack's words, 'divisive, actor-oriented, explosive rather than organic'. But this is far from the kind of sentimental reading which would hope to claim the elitist Ben unambiguously for the 'people'. It is the very strictness of Jonson's classicism which makes him hypersensitive to the 'anarchic and unverifiable plurality of the vernacular'; and if he can be spoken of as 'carnivalesque', it is a carnival of the criminal underworld, rather than one of unqualified festive liberation. Only the astonishing libertine riot of *Bartholemew Fair* escapes to some extent from this stricture, adhering to the classical unities with such pedantic tenacity that it succeeds only in making a mockery of them.

In its subtle interweaving of textual analysis, social history, cultural theory and, above all, a magnificent sense of theatre, Peter Womack's study rescues Ben Jonson simultaneously from the classical humanists and the romantic populists. It delivers us – instead – a Jonson who is not only readable, but usable, for our own times.

Terry Eagleton

Preface

Despite much lip-service, the literary criticism of classic plays still pays surprisingly little attention to their function as scripts for the theatre. One of the aims of this book is to question that prevailing habit of abstraction. I have therefore, regretfully, neglected Jonson's nondramatic poetry so as to be able to concentrate on the plays.

With the needs of students in mind, I have made moderate assumptions about the amount my reader knows. Familiarity with the three undisputed masterpieces – *Volpone*, *The Alchemist* and *Bartholomew Fair* — is all that is essential. Beyond these, it would also be useful to have read (in descending order of usefulness) *Catiline*, *Epicoene*, *Every Man in His Humour*, *The Devil Is An Ass*, *Every Man Out Of His Humour*, *Sejanus* and the rest. In drawing on the less well-known texts, I've tried to write descriptively, so as not to lose a reader who doesn't know them at first hand.

I would like to thank, for various kinds of help, Philip Carpenter, Sarah Carpenter, Julie Curtis, Terry Eagleton, Wendy Greenhill, Jane Holdsworth, Helen Lockyer, Ray Ockenden and Charles Swann. I'm also grateful for the patience with which my wife, my daughter, and my colleagues at Strode College have absorbed Jonson as an alien and time-consuming intruder in their lives. My longest-standing acknowledgement, an impersonal one, is to the company of Trevor Nunn's RSC production of *The Alchemist* at The Other

Place, Stratford and the Aldwych Theatre, London, 1977–8. The vicious and euphoric entertainment they made of the play on the stage is the real object of the theoretical enquiry that follows.

1 Speaking

Whatever else a playwright may be doing, he is making up things for actors to say. Here are two examples, first spoken in 1610 and 1611 respectively:

Subtle   Thou vermin, have I ta'en thee, out of dung,
        So poor, so wretched, when no living thing
        Would keep thee company, but a spider, or
          worse?
        Raised thee from brooms, and dust and watering-
          pots?
        Sublimed thee, and exalted thee, and fixed thee
        I'the third region, called our state of grace?
        Wrought thee to spirit, to quintessence, with pains
        Would twice have won me the philosophers' work?
        Put thee in words and fashion? Made thee fit
        For more than ordinary fellowships?
        Given thee thy oaths, thy quarrelling dimensions?
        Thy rules, to cheat at horse-race; cock-pit, cards,
        Dice, or whatever gallant tincture else?
        Made thee a second in mine own great art?
        And have I this for thank? Do you rebel?
        Do you fly out, i' the projection?
                            (Alchemist, I.i.64–78)

> *Miranda*   I pitied thee,
>   Took pains to make thee speak, taught thee each
>   hour
>   One thing or other. When thou didst not, savage,
>   Know thine own meaning, but wouldst gabble like
>   A thing most brutish, I endow'd thy purposes
>   With words that made them known. But thy vile
>   race,
>   Though thou didst learn, had that in't which good
>   natures
>   Could not abide to be with; therefore wast thou
>   Deservedly confin'd into this rock, who hadst
>   Deserv'd more than a prison.[1]

In both speeches, a teacher is reproaching a pupil for his ingratitude. Both teachers claim to have taught their pupils to speak and, for both, this is not just a matter of imparting a skill, but a transformation of the pupil's being, an upward passage out of a gross and subhuman condition. Both contexts associate this transformation with 'art', that union of knowledge and power which at its highest pitch, as expounded by Subtle and by the listening Prospero, takes the form of magic. The speeches are also very similar from the point of view of dramatic technique: both use the speaker's resentment to motivate an exposition of something which is supposed to have happened before the beginning of the play.

Within that common framework of Renaissance ideas and dramatic function, though, the speeches work very differently. Miranda speaks at a consistent level of moderate abstraction: her nouns are almost all the names of ideas, but of quite commonplace ideas, which don't require her to deviate from the language of ordinary conversation. Subtle has that register too, including several of the same words, but his vocabulary also ascends to the celestial ('spirit', 'grace') and descends to the brooms and the cock-pit. It's not just a contrast between high and low styles, but equally one between the general and the particular: the 'third region' is a term in cosmology, part of a language for describing the entire universe, while the point of the reference to spiders and watering-pots is that, before he met Subtle, Face was working as the caretaker in his employer's deserted house. (Thus 'dust', for instance, is a sort of interstylistic pun: it's both the alchemical opposite of quintessence, the lowest as opposed to the highest form of matter, and a flatly specific reminder that in his previous existence Face was doing the dusting.) The effect, in contrast with the even tenor of Miranda's expression, is of a violent linguistic switchback, alternating between the most refined ideas and the most blankly material contingencies.

This is in line with the two speakers' theories of *how* speech, imparted with such pains, effects the transition from a lower to a higher form of life. For Miranda, it's a question of *ending* a state of alienation: whereas, before, Caliban was cut off from his 'own meaning' by his inarticulacy, now his 'purposes' can be known, to himself and others. Speech heals the rift between the creature and itself; it enables us to become integral and actual; in one word, it is natural. (This isn't how it feels to Caliban, of course, but the speech has 'confin'd' that contradiction by referring it to something in his 'race'.) Subtle, on the other hand, has taken Face from a minimal but self-sufficient state and 'put him in words' as into fancy dress, giving him access to the multiple distractions and deceptions the speech torrentially enumerates. So far from constituting nature, words are a gaudy means of going beyond it. What is actual – this is of course given in the terms of the plot – is not an outcome of the process of learning to speak, but the wretched pre-linguistic isolation which was its starting point. Speech supplements and disintegrates.

This divisiveness is written deep into the structure of the rhetoric. 'Have I ...' in line 64 starts a rhetorical question whose sense is not completed until line 77, the closure being delayed by a sequence of eight participial phrases in parallel dependence on the opening verb. Individual items on this monstrous list sprout their own sub-lists: 'Sublimed thee, and exalted thee, and fixed thee', 'horse-race, cock-pit, cards, /

Dice', and so on. Unlike Miranda's speech, which has the sequential logic of a story, Subtle's has no internal principle which could control its length: he will just go on until he runs out of fingers to number his points on. The only principle is enumeration – that's to say, a representational arrangement which establishes no relationship between its elements; an order that doesn't mean anything. It sets up tensions in the speech because the unresolved heterogeneity of objects is constantly threatening to subvert the intentional unity proposed by the syntax. The peculiar tone that results is a distinctive Jonsonian mark; it's set, for example, on what Jonson takes from Marlowe's style, an appropriation first noted by T.S. Eliot.[2] Eliot illustrates his election of Jonson as Marlowe's 'legitimate heir' by quoting Sir Epicure Mammon:

> I will have all my beds, blown up; not stuffed:
> Down is too hard. And then, mine oval room,
> Filled with such pictures, as Tiberius took
> From Elephantis, and dull Aretine
> But coldly imitated. Then, my glasses,
> Cut in more subtle angles, to disperse
> And multiply the figures, as I walk
> Naked between my *succubae*.
>
> (*Alchemist*, II.ii.41–8)

The poetry of boundless acquisitiveness, spanning ages and continents, certainly recalls, say, the opening soliloquy from *The Jew of Malta*, or Faustus' anticipation of what he will do with his infernal slaves. But Marlowe's sustained line, the bravura of a tyrannical subjectivity ceaselessly realizing itself in the spoils of the world, gets snagged at every point. The inflatatable beds, the up-market pornography, and the trick mirrors are at once too minutely imagined and too nearly feasible for their hyperbolic function: they stick in their own eccentric particularity and refuse to be subordinated to the generalized image of infinite riches. As in Subtle's speech, the successive units are participial phrases each referring back to the opening verb; together with the naive connectives ('And then ... Then ...') this gives the dream of the stone an incongruously itemizing character. Unconfined desire is displaced into a global shopping list.

Even when Subtle's rhetorical question is finally completed, the enumerating frenzy isn't exhausted. 'And have I this for thank?' is immediately followed by two more questions which are, so to speak, in apposition to it. Face's behaviour is thus denounced in three separate formulas: personal, political and alchemical. This is another Jonsonian figure, not exactly the same as the list, but closely related to it, and no less characteristic. It consists of gratuitously offering more than one way of saying the same thing. There's a good example in Mammon's speech when his pictures are said to be like Tiberius', and also to be better than Aretine's. The semantic difference between the two similes is negligible: the extra comparison is a reflex, not of doubt or scrupulous exactness, but of accumulation. *Volpone* is full of such gestures. Volpone's gold shows:

> ... like a flame by night; or like the day
> Struck out of chaos
>
> (I.i.8–9)

Promising Volpone's gratitude to Corbaccio, Mosca declares:

> He cannot be stupid, or stone dead . . .
>
> (I.iv.107)

Mosca says of Celia:

> All her looks are sweet,
> As the first grapes or cherries
>
> (I.v.120–1)

Corvino, in his jealousy of the mountebank, sarcastically promises Celia:

> He shall come home and minister unto you
> The fricace for the mother. Or, let me see,
> I think you'd rather mount; would you not mount?
>
> (II.v.16–18)

The figure can be inflected differently in different contexts, but the general effect of its repetition is to open up further possibilities of indefinitely additive speech (if there are two formulas, there's no reason why there shouldn't be more), and at the same time to denaturalize the metaphoric connection (the content of the trope is visibly chosen, arbitrary, inorganic). Like Mammon's mirrors, words are so arranged as to disperse and multiply the intention that seeks to command them.

If Miranda's style, then, manifests the unity of an integral speaking subject, Subtle's speech characteristically disintegrates its subject by its own indiscriminate supplementarity. In the terms of realistic theatre, the simple way of putting that would be to say that Miranda is sane and Subtle is crazy. This is by no means a hopeless misconception: we certainly miss one of the vital sources of hilarity and danger in Jonson's entertainments if we pretend not to notice that in each of his major plays the action is initiated by someone – Sejanus, Volpone, Morose, Catiline, Overdo – who is, as John Arden says, as cracked as an old carrot.[3] But this is not a formulation that tells us as much as it seems to. After all, it's obvious that we can't really attribute the structures of a theatrical text to the state of mind of its characters. Rather, the characters' having minds at all is an optical illusion generated by the structures of the text. So what we want to know about is the textual (linguistic, theatrical, ideological) pressure that repeatedly cracks the carrot. To put it another way: it's quite easy to show that in Jonson the theatrical word is conflictual in character. But what is the conflict *about*?

In his essay 'From the prehistory of novelistic discourse', M.M. Bakhtin argues that traditional stylistics has been a contemplation of the 'direct poetic word' – the word, that is, from which meaning, object and theme are inseparable, so that the poet experiences himself directly in his own language. Against, and outside, this primary means of representing the world, Bakhtin sets a quite distinct discourse, which he regards as characteristic and constitutive of the novel – that which adopts language, not simply as an instrument of representation, but also as an object of representation. This indirect word lends itself to parody, to presentation at one remove, to utterance in 'intonational quotation marks'; it particularizes and frames *the image of another's speech*, and so relativizes the conjunction of language and reality, discovering the capacity of the object to give rise, not just to one verbal representation, but to an indefinite number of different ones.[4]

Bakhtin calls discourse which is innocent of all such quotation marks *monologic*. Pure monologism is strictly speaking inconceivable, because language is constitutively a matter of dialogue; there is no kind of utterance which does not in some way take up a previous one, look out for a subsequent counter-word, and negotiate with competing contexts for control of its semantic units. But it's still meaningful to talk about the monologic word, because there are forms of discourse which converge on such a state – which lack, or are designed to suppress, all awareness of their own latent dialogism. In literature, for example, the high genres – epic, tragedy – legislate to purify the word and create a field where language and meaning coincide in a unitary and authoritative fashion.

In its simplest form, 'novelistic' discourse subverts such unitary languages (literary or otherwise) by parodying them, that is, it ridicules their claims to completeness by representing them as objects and so exposing their 'bounded' reality. This doesn't exactly produce dialogue, because the object-language is simply inverted as a whole; transformed, in its new ironic context, from pure signifier to pure signified. Fielding's *Shamela* would be an example of this extremely limited dialogic mode. A much more dynamic situation arises when the 'speech of the other', despite being stylized, permeated by the parodying consciousness of the author, nevertheless retains its ability to represent the world. When this happens, what is produced is no longer simply an image of speech, but an image that speaks, a represented representation which can, as Bakhtin puts it, have arguments with the authorial discourse. 'The author represents this language, carries on a conversation with it, and the conversation penetrates into the interior of this language-image and dialogizes it from within.'[5] To take a one-word example, the impersonal narrator in *Bleak House* speaks of Sir Leicester Dedlock's 'magnificence'. Taken as a direct word, this term would just be the narrator's name for certain qualities (splendour, greatness of mind, etc.) which the character is supposed to possess. That, for instance, is how the same word is used in *Paradise Lost*, when the sky is imagined as speaking 'the Makers high magnificence'.[6] Not that it is devoid of ambivalence in this epic and monologic context, for there is heavenly magnificence, which is spacious and wise, and satanic magnificence, which is gorgeous and monarchical; but in neither case is there any sign that the word has been borrowed from the speech of another, or is anything other than a direct representation of its object. Dickens, by contrast, puts the word in contexts which make its referent seem incongruously concrete and quantifiable ('Not a little more magnificence, therefore, on the part of Sir Leicester'; 'Sir Leicester's magnificence explodes').[7] The narrator has, as it were, found the term in the vocabulary of somebody else – not Sir Leicester, but some uncritical admirer of the aristocratic values he represents – and taken it over without fully making it his own. As a result, it does serve his descriptive intention (this is not just a naively ironic intimation that Sir Leicester isn't really magnificent at all), but he is using it without conviction, and getting it slightly wrong. This wrongness is the point of entry by which authorial intonations penetrate the represented word and dialogize it.

Bakhtin maintains that the protean possibilities of internal dialogization are fully worked out only in the novel: it's above all in Rabelais, Cervantes, Sterne, Pushkin, Dickens and Dostoevsky that authorial and represented languages intersect, infect one another, and pull the word towards contrary language centres. But the novel in this sense has a rich prehistory, and even from my account of it, abstracted from the literary-historical content of Bakhtin's analysis, it should be clear that this is to be found in low and mixed types of writing – in satire, travesty, antimasque, farce, burlesque, abuse. The type of writing, in fact, of which Jonson's theatrical output is, among other things, a vast and sophisticated compendium.

A relatively clear-cut example of Jonson's procedures is provided by a passage in *Sejanus*. Macro, having been commissioned by Tiberius to work under cover against Sejanus, has a soliloquy which begins:

> I will not ask, why Caesar bids do this:
> But joy, that he bids me. It is the bliss
> Of courts, to be employed; no matter, how:
> A prince's power makes all his actions virtue.
> We, whom he works by, are dumb instruments,
> To do but not enquire: his great intents
> Are to be served, not searched. Yet, as that bow
> Is most in hand, whose owner best doth know
> T' affect his aims, so let that statesman hope
> Most use, most price, can hit his prince's scope.
> Nor must he look at what, or whom to strike,
> But loose at all; each mark must be alike.
>
> (Sejanus, III,714–25)

Macro is expressing his readiness to be used, to make himself into a 'dumb instrument' of state power. His speech therefore compares interestingly with an epigram Jonson wrote about the same issue, 'On Spies':

> Spies, you are lights in state, but of base stuff,
> Who, when you have burnt yourselves down to the snuff,
> Stink, and are thrown away. End fair enough.
>
> (Epigrams, LIX)

The force of the epigram comes from the precision and speed with which it generates double meanings. The comparison of

spies and candles is proposed in a form which is complimentary to the spies, but this courtesy is instantly coun-
tered by four further grounds of comparison, all of them
disgraceful: the metaphor turns out to be two-edged. More
subtly, the minor and utilitarian character of the 'vehicle'
makes an independent dismissive comment: the spies
resemble candles not only in shedding light on things, con-
suming themselves, and so on, but also in being cheap articles
in everyday use. So the equation between men and utensils,
which at first looked as if it was merely the mechanism of the
epigram, ends up as part of its point. But both of these shifts
(in the value the analogy carries, and in the level at which it
operates) are witty – that's to say, they're executed under the
control of a single speaker, a single consciousness, albeit one
who may have a complex attitude towards state informers
(they're useful and despicable). The very tightness of the
control ensures that the double meanings don't amount to a
double language.

The simile of the bow in Macro's speech has the same kind
of wit playing over it. At first the comparison between the
man and the weapon looks like a mere expository device:
statesmen resemble bows in that the ones which serve their
masters most accurately are the most frequently employed
and command the highest price. But then the equation turns
out to be the point, not just the means, of the exposition.
Service involves being owned and used, not having preferences
of one's own – in short, not just resembling a certain thing
in certain ways, as a lady might resemble a rose, but actually
becoming a thing. So far the logic is just like that of the epigram.
But of course it isn't possible for a speaker to represent himself
as an object in that consistent way: the analogy is damaged
by the fact that he is expounding it. So if Macro is becoming
a thing, the speech is also full of the consciousness which is
doing the becoming; tensely not asking, not enquiring, not
searching. Under this pressure the simile collapses into
absurdity: lines 723–5, taken together, amount to the demand
that the perfect statesman should hit the right target without

looking at it. As the tropical language breaks up, words fall out of it into more literal significations: 'affect his aims' and 'hit his scope' seem to imply a conscious executive function which further invalidates the objectification of the agent; while the excess of archery verbs – 'hit', 'strike', 'loose', 'mark' – with the ominous 'what, or whom' carry the reference beyond the rules of the comparison out to the real murders of Tiberian (and Jacobean) politics. Thus the epigrammatic word, taken out of its generic abstraction and plunged into internal dialogue with the language of another, can no longer thematize directly the reason of state, but struggles instead with its irrationality.

The language of the other, the monologic *court word*, is stylized in the earlier part of the speech in religious terms. Macro's election by the emperor is 'joy', and 'bliss'; and it's by a devotional logic that he concludes that whatever his master does is of heaven. Tiberius is God (his deification is, in fact, a live political issue in the world of the play), and true virtue consists in perfect submission to his will. The reverent tone of the next sentence bears out the theological imagery. But the coherence of that cosmology is all 'inside' the court word – in exaggerating its grandiloquence through the lofty generalizations and sententious couplets, in laying the vocabulary open to the Machiavellian connotations of 'prince' and 'great' and the coarse colloquial ones of 'employed' and 'do', and above all in naming the language–image itself, with a rhythmic pause just beforehand to move the tone towards bathos ('It is the bliss – of courts'), the writing penetrates Macro's speech with parodic authorial intonations. Yet the parody is not necessarily simple. About two years after the first performance of *Sejanus*, one of the speakers in Jonson's first court masque could describe Britain as

> Ruled by a sun that to this height doth grace it,
> Whose beams shine day and night, and are of force
> To blanch an Ethiop, and revive a corse.

His light sciential is, and, past mere nature,
Can salve the rude defects of every creature.
                    (*Masque of Blackness*, 223–7)

The supernatural sun is the watching King James. Macro's theology of power will not separate itself out from the authorial language as a clearly bounded object of representation; it's the (polemical) image of a language the author is also able to speak. But on the public stage, presented at one remove from the highly authoritarian univocality of the court itself, it is dialogized.

A brief survey of the idea of 'making' in the play shows the process at work. When Macro says that a prince's power makes all his actions virtue, does that mean, cynically, that the power makes the actions pass for virtue, or that the prince really does have power over moral categories? It would be consistent, at least, with what I've said so far to take it that Macro, inside the theological discourse of the court, is using the word in the second sense, while the authorial (epigrammatic) discourse counters it with the first. In the first doubtful use of the word in the play, though, the implications are different again. Silius, who, as a virtuous and semi-choric figure more or less speaks in the style of a Juvenalian satiric commentator, denounces informers who

Flatter, and swear, forswear, deprave, inform,
Smile, and betray; make guilty men ....
                                          (I.28–9)

The other verbs make it clear that the spies are also *agents provocateurs* – they really do 'make guilty', not just 'make seem guilty'. If anything, Silius' usage strengthens the 'court' side of the semantic argument. Ironically, it's Tiberius himself who later confronts that sense with a morality outside the court theology. Sejanus advises him to kill the opponents he fears:

Tiberius That nature, blood, and laws of kind forbid.
Sejanus Do policy, and state forbid it?
Tiberius No.
Sejanus The rest of poor respects, then, let go by:
State is enough to make th'act just, them guilty.

(II.170–3)

Here at the top, where the making is actually done, the awareness obtrudes that guilt and innocence are terms in other languages too, and the word moves back towards its limited, cynical form. Elsewhere, later on in the soliloquy of Macro's already quoted, the word is again used on the boundary of the court discourse, but instead of introducing doubt, the shadow of the alternative context is the occasion of a violent rejection:

Were it to … work all my kin
To swift perdition; leave no untrained engine,
For friendship, or for innocence; nay, make
The gods all guilty: I would undertake
This, being imposed me …

(III.726–34)

Macro here denies the resistance to his discourse suggested by 'kin', 'friendship', 'innocence', 'the gods': it's the most absolute claim in the play for the sovereignty of the prince's 'making' power. But its terms defeat themselves: an intersecting authorial intonation classifies the project of making the gods guilty as a logical absurdity, a silly thing to say. Macro is 'placed' – but the placing is itself challenged by the fact that in the play's climactic *coup de théâtre* Tiberius, operating from Capreae through Macro himself, first raises Sejanus to the height of virtue and then 'makes him guilty' by the delphic ambiguities of his letter to the Senate. Thus, throughout the play, the validity of the court sense of 'make' can never be conclusively accepted or rejected.

We should be clear that this is not simply a type of ambiguity. Authorially, there is no doubt at all in the play that virtue is virtue, and guilt guilt, and no-one has the power to alter these categories. People may speak as if someone does, but they're wrong. However, the monologic speech in which that conviction can be made to stick is subverted by the dialogizing forces activated by the 'making' of the drama. The epigrammatist gets involved in an unwise conversation.

To construct the participants of that conversation, it will be useful to recall our opening principle – that playwrights are people who write things for actors to say – and try to see the mode of production of theatrical speech as a whole.

The essential context of Jonson's work is London, where he was born and where, almost exclusively, he was performed and published. During his lifetime, the city was becoming a metropolis. Its estimated population increased from 150,000 to 350,000 – at once a total enormously higher than that of the next largest town in Britain, and a growth rate several times faster than that of the national population. It also acquired a significant seasonal population because the centralization of royal and legal administration brought the provincial ruling class 'up to Town' (the significant locution begins at about this time). This very great concentration of people, wealth and power was also a focus for the poor, the unattached, the ambitious – 'masterless men' whose urban and individualistic mode of social existence was as destructive of feudal rhythms as the mercantile dynamism of the city. These conditions made possible a type of theatrical organization in which acting companies, though they were still nominally and legally the 'servants' of an aristocratic patron, in fact operated by venturing capital on buildings, performers, decor and scripts, and making their profit at the box office. This form of theatre took shape in the 1570s (that is, in Jonson's infancy), and by the later 1590s, when he began writing for the stage, there were two well-established companies run on such lines, with competition from other more transitory organizations. In 1599–1600, just after Jonson's first success as a playwright, two children's companies reappeared on the market, and through the rest of his career, on any normal weekday afternoon, something like half a dozen commercial theatres would be playing, to a maximum capacity of about 10,000. For the first time in history, theatre was regularly operating as a capitalist industry. The shares were owned by a restricted group of actors, who hired other adult actors as waged workers, and boys (needed, of course, for female roles) as apprentices.[8]

This development exposed the theatrical word to an audience which had no externally given homogeneity. Whereas medieval religious theatre had consciously played to a community of the faithful, and even the professional performers of Tudor interludes had probably addressed, most of the time, the extended households of the great men or corporations who hired them, the purpose-built theatres opened their doors to anyone who paid, which seems to have included not only noblemen, gentlemen and students, but also, according to the Lord Mayor of London, 'vagrant persons & maisterles men that hang about the Citie, theeves, horsestealers, whoremoongers, coozeners, connycatching persones, practizers of treason, & such other lyke'.[9] An inorganic audience of this kind, in the linguistic and class conditions of Elizabethan England, must be, in Bakhtin's word, *heteroglot* – not a constituency to which a unitary or authoritative word could be addressed from the stage. Jonson summarizes the situation very accurately in his translation of the *Ars Poetica*:

>   alas, what knew
> The idiot, keeping holiday, or drudge,
> Clown, townsman, base, and noble, mixed, to judge?
> Thus, to his ancient art the piper lent
> Gesture, and riot, whilst he swooping went
> In his trained gown about the stage: so grew
> In time to tragedy, a music new.
> The rash, and headlong eloquence brought forth
> Unwonted language; and that sense of worth
> That found out profit, and foretold each thing,

Now differed not from Delphic riddling.
(Horace, of the Art of Poetry, 300–10)

The casual and heterogeneous character of the new urban audience breaks the traditional constraints on both staging and language; the direct word, spoken in the assembly of a knowable community –

not yet

So over-thick, but, where the people met,
They might with ease be numbered

(291–3)

– is displaced by novelty and ambiguity. Language no longer arises naturally from the object, but takes on an autonomous and exhibitionistic life beyond it. In the juridical and pedagogic categories of the text this development necessarily appears as a triumph of anarchy and ignorance – but then Jonson's poem, both as a didactic epistle and as a translated classic, is an instance of precisely the type of authoritative word whose failure to hold the stage it describes.

The heteroglossia[10] of the mixed audience was not, however, the only context of the word in the theatre. Although the actors lived by the paying audience, they did so under the authorization of the royal government. The administration of the City of London was on the whole hostile to the theatre (largely, it seems, for reasons of public order), and it was the power of the court which protected it from harassment or even closure. One price of this protection was acceptance of a strict censorship: all new scripts were read by the Master of the Revels and performed under his licence. The companies also acted frequently at court, drawing from their ordinary commercial repertoire. On the accession of James I, these royal connections were formalized by taking the patronage of theatre companies out of the hands of the aristocracy and distributing it among the members of the royal family. It's not clear that this change made a great deal of practical difference, but it must have increased the visibility of the relationship. It coincided with a gradual shift in the centre of theatrical gravity from the big unroofed playhouses on the south bank of the river to 'private' houses in the liberties of the City, which were smaller, more expensive, and candle-lit. Jonson was writing for a theatre which was moving, socially, politically and stylistically, deeper into the ambience of royal absolutism; and when, five years after his death, the absolutism was politically defeated, the theatre went down too. But the incorporation was never completed, and in 1615 – the year after the double première of *Bartholomew Fair* (one day on Bankside and the next day at court) – it could still be said of the actor that 'howsoever hee pretends to have a royall Master or Mistresse, his wages and dependance prove him to be the servant of the people.'[11] The Jacobean theatre continued to address itself to two audiences, one diverse, the other unitary – the public, and the king.

Within this hybrid the situation of the writer varied somewhat from case to case. The underlying relationship was one of simple commodity production: the writer sold a physical manuscript to the company, whose property it then became. Rates were such that it was possible to make a reasonable living (probably quite a lot more than a schoolmaster or a non-theatrical writer) by selling about two plays a year. The reason for this was the theatre's pressing demand for scripts: with most of the texts of the previous century rendered unusable by revolutionary changes, not only in the constitution of the audience, but also in the prevailing religious orthodoxy, the companies had no stock of past plays; it's likely, moreover, that they were playing to a limited public which came often, so that even very successful plays didn't have many performances by modern standards. The actors couldn't afford to be without new – and novel – scripts in large numbers, and people who could provide what they needed were in an economic position stronger than that of most literary producers before the enactment of authorial copyright. In practice, though, writers were often more closely attached to companies than that suggests: a writer would often place a whole run of plays with the same company, also engaging in collaborations or rewrites for them. The advantages of such a link – sometimes cemented by the writer doing some acting too – are clear enough: the writer gained some security from association with one of the centres of power in the industry, and the company got scripts which were tailored to the requirements of its own performers and audiences. There was consequently a tendency, recognizable from other kinds of early capitalist production, for the relationship of buyer and seller to harden into that of employer and wage-earner. One writer in the 1630s was retained on a contract which guaranteed him a weekly salary in return for exclusive rights on a set number of scripts he engaged to produce. Almost certainly there were other such contracts which don't happen to have been preserved.[12]

It's important to bear in mind, then, that both Shakespeare and Jonson had economically untypical careers, deviating in opposite ways from a normal relationship with the means of production. Shakespeare was a shareholder himself: he wrote all his plays for the company of which he was also an acting member and part owner. He therefore had a uniquely close relationship with a single organization, but was not in any sense its employee; rather, the contradictions latent in the productive relations were simply abolished by his personally uniting the different roles that made them up. Jonson, on the other hand, seems never, until the very end of his career, to have written more than two consecutive plays for the same company; moreover, after an initial period of perhaps five years (1597–1601) when the theatre was his sole source of income, he never produced enough scripts for him to be thought of as a fully professional theatre writer. He said in 1619 that all his plays together hadn't brought him £200[13]: at less than £10 a year, that would be enough to survive on, but very low earnings for the theatre, and not enough to support Jonson's expensive social and literary involvements. In other words he was, deliberately, a part-time playwright. So we can say, schematically, that he and Shakespeare both avoided the incipient proletarianizing of the writer by the theatre – Shakespeare by integrating himself into the institution, and Jonson by withholding himself from it. This corresponds rather closely with the contrasting styles of speech they provide for actors.

Jonson's detachment was made possible by the existence of three alternative centres of literary production: masque writing for the court; literary patronage; and publication.

Masques were probably the most significant of these as far as making a living was concerned. Regular commissions for court celebrations between 1605 and 1625 brought Jonson uncertain but probably quite lavish rewards, and also gave him privileged access to court circles for most of the reign of James I, so creating the social conditions for what Herford and Simpson call 'the heyday of his personal dictatorship in the literary world'[14] – the decade 1616–25. These were also the years in which he wrote no plays for the theatre at all. I shall have more to say about the masques later on; the immediate point about them is that here the theatrical word is systematically integrated with the single occasion on which it is spoken. The royal spectators and their dependants are drawn into the stage language as symbols, dancers and addressees, but at the same time that particular and complimental relationship is forced into universality by an elaborate allegorization. The monoglot assembly to which the direct word can be spoken is reconstructed by royal *fiat*; heteroglossia is suppressed by an authority which is in every sense arbitrary.

Masques transfigured the body of the state: patronage served as its nervous system, its means at once of reproducing its own cohesion and of exercising control over civil society. It was, ambiguously, a vast mechanism of bribery and corruption and a sort of demilitarized feudalism, whereby a wide range of administrative and ideological functions, including literature, were organized, not according to a generalized model of state employment, but in particularized relationships of personal favour and service.[15] For poetry, the important thing about this structure is the individual orientation it gives to writing: the occasional address to a patron or a dedicatee centres the word on a known reader who is approached according to known rules of etiquette. This social specification is not confined to dedication and encomium strictly defined, but extends to epithalamion, elegy, love poetry and – a significant category for Jonson – commendatory verses prefixed to the works of other writers. Almost all Jonson's non-dramatic verse is in some variety of this personal mode. Even satire is touched by the distinctive orientation: the *Epigrams* mingle laudatory addresses to named persons with derogatory addresses to unnamed ones, so that the latter appear as inverted dedications or travestied epitaphs.

The ties of friendship or duty retain the word and create the practical conditions for the image of a language which closes unambiguously on its meanings. 'An Epistle to Master John Selden' both describes and exploits the possibilities. It begins:

> I know to whom I write. Here, I am sure,
> Though I am short, I cannot be obscure:
> Less shall I for the art or dressing care;
> Truth, and the Graces, best when naked are.
>
> (Underwoods, XIV,1–4)

Despite the absolute air of the last line, the explicit placing of the style in its occasion makes it clear that the nakedness of truth is not a universally available condition, but a rare opportunity gained by writing 'here', in the front matter of a friend's book. Personal familiarity within a shared code (stylishly implied by the casual allusion to Horace – 'brevis esse laboro, obscurus fio')[16] provides a special medium in which language and reality meet. Reader and, correspondingly, writer become visible in the text, whose validity is therefore underwritten by the good faith of their relationship. A little later, Jonson confesses that he has bestowed undeserved praise in the past, and continues

Since being deceived, I turn a sharper eye
Upon myself, and ask to whom, and why,
And what I write? And vex it many days
Before men get a verse: much less a praise;
So that my reader is assured, I now
Mean what I speak: and still will keep that vow.
Stand forth my object, then ....

(23–9)

It's by providing extremely limited and concrete answers to
the author's internal questions that the commendatory form
confirms the related integrity of speaker, meaning and object.
Conversely, the achieved integrity constitutes a space in which
the questions can be formulated in this exceptionally plain
and referential style. But certainly the limits are drastic, and
the differences that press against them – facility, 'dressing', a
muse 'smelling parasite'[17] – are insistently present in the
language which keeps them at bay.

All these forms of production – plays for the public stage,
masques for the court, poems addressed to individuals within
the grammar of patronage – were also, in the second place,
meant for publication. Print is for Jonson the definitive form
of the word, the unifying term of a teleology which renders
his commitment to all its primary contexts partial and tran-
sitional. In this he deviates sharply from the theory and
practice of most contemporary playwrights. Companies, on
the whole, were reluctant to see their plays in print until their
box office potential was more or less exhausted, and although
they had no automatic power to stop a writer selling his work
to the booksellers if he really wanted to, there were several
reasons why he might not press the point. Playbooks were
regarded as a trivial and ephemeral form of literature unlikely
to attract the patronage which was a more significant reward
of authorship than sales; good houses and good relations with
the company counted for more than such dubious benefits;
there was perhaps even a feeling that to sell the same manuscript twice for two different kinds of reproduction would be

dishonourable.[18] Besides, the organizational subordination of writers to actors tended to support an aesthetic judgement that the life of a play was on the stage, and the printed script no more than its memorial.[19] Shakespeare's famous lack of interest in the publication of his plays (contrasted with his careful presentation of his narrative poems) is, as might be predicted from his peculiar position, wholly in line with these principles. Jonson, on the other hand, not only edited his plays for separate quarto publication – in one or two cases even revising and annotating them – but also produced, in 1616, a collected edition in folio, with a grandiose title page full of emblematic figures and announcing *The Works of Benjamin Jonson*. Three-quarters of the space in these 'Works' was occupied by plays, a paradox which was not then merely verbal.[20]

Jonson's authorization for this startling departure was clearly classical drama, Renaissance editions of which were the model for his own. The book is a gesture beyond its own time, both placing its author in the same light as the playwrights of antiquity and providing the means for him to be appreciated, like them, by posterity. In a simultaneous and closely related move, it appeals from the collective audience to the solitary reader. The motto makes this explicit:

> neque, me ut miretur turba, laboro:
> contentus paucis lectoribus.[21]

The reader's value, like that of posterity, is a function of his opposition to the immediate, heterogeneous crowd, where each spectator's judgement is distorted by the influence of the people around him.[22] The singleness of his encounter with the text guarantees the unity of the voice that addresses him, its utterances abstracted from their diverse practical contexts and gathered together under the sign of authorship.

The force of that opposition can be felt in the unusual insistence with which Jonson addresses the reader in the prefaces to *Catiline* and *The New Inn*, the two plays of his which were disastrous failures with audiences. Introducing the latter, he has recourse from the fashionable prejudices of the Blackfriars spectators to the 'rustic candour' of the reader – yet another formula for his remoteness. For *Catiline*, Jonson produced a strange sequence of three prefatory addresses. The first, a dedication to the Lord Chamberlain, includes the declaration: 'Posterity may pay your benefit the honour and thanks, when it shall know, that you dare, in these jig-given times, to countenance a legitimate Poem' (2.5). This is the appeal to the future again, and also the dichotomy of reader and spectator in the form of an emphatic separation between the play as theatre and as literature. (Jigs, the vulgar song-and-dance farces given in most playhouses as afterpieces, are pointed up here as the most clearly non-literary aspect of the theatre.) The second address teasingly informs 'the Reader in Ordinary' that Jonson cares nothing for the ill-informed censure he expects from him 'whom I see already busy with the title, and tricking over the leaves: it is your own. I departed with my right, when I first let it abroad'. (1–3). And the third, 'To the Reader Extraordinary', says only: 'You I would understand to be the better man, though places in court go otherwise: to you I submit myself and work. Farewell' (1–2). So the preface as a whole bewilderingly multiplies the reader whose singleness was just the reason for turning to him. The second address parodies the ideal of a direct encounter between writer and reader by its whimsical pretence that Jonson is literally there on the page, watching us. The third one undermines the second by taking back its declaration of commercial indifference, and also takes a side-swipe at the code of patronage which is the basis of the first. The appeal beyond the crowd dissolves in a troubling play of ironies, reproducing the discursive instability it's meant to transcend. The reason, I think, is that Jonson is here trying not so much to contact an actual reader as to construct the 'virtual public'[23] – that notional 'everyone' which is predicated by publication itself, and whose attention is able to confer universal significance on the words it reads. If that's so, then, ironically, Jonson's classicizing rejection of the theatre fulfils the logic of his relations with it as a producer. For this universal, value-awarding reader, innocent of time and place, free of all the historical constraints which could distort his reception of the text, is distinctly recognizable as that general requirement of commodity production, the consumer.

When we speak, then, about Jonson's 'authorial discourse', what we mean is not in the least the spontaneous expression of his personal feelings, but a complex stylistic construction, the overdetermined[24] hypostasization of several productive relationships. In a way, it's a cunning project of freedom: the stance of the commercial playwright, able to earn his living in the market place, counters the sycophancy which threatens the identity of the literary protegé;[25] the role of servant of kings is protection from the risks and humiliations of being just a popular entertainer;[26] the language of the familiar epistle inhibits the totalizing claims of the allegory of state – and the author comes into view as that which reserves to itself the power of *choosing* between these competing linguistic embodiments. Even the *Works* are not coterminous with this figure, since Jonson wrote almost nothing which doesn't have a primary occasion of some kind: the reader always gets him second.

Biographically, this reservation can be derived from the forces which placed Jonson outside the institutions of literary production I've been sketching. The son of an impoverished clergyman, and stepson of a bricklayer, he was placed in Westminster School by an unknown benefactor and then, at some point in his teens, taken out of school and put into a craft apprenticeship. He soon abandoned that, and there followed about a decade of which almost nothing is known. It seems that he was a volunteer in the war in Flanders for a time, and it's likely, from the erudition of his earliest surviving work, that he was pursuing a classical education on his own account. He was, in short, one of that marginalized class, with more education than opportunities of employment, which is idealized and anathematized in his own plays and those of his contemporaries in the figure of the malcontent;

the trace, at once alienated and enlivening, of the over-
production of intellectuals.[27] His initiation into literary culture thus spoiled him for a bricklayer without integrating him
into the social systems which administered it. (It did have
the ideologically less nuanced advantage of saving his life,
when he used his Latin to claim benefit of clergy after killing
a man in a fight.) He didn't go to university or the inns of
court; his on-and-off relations with the capitalists of the theatre we've seen; his background wasn't fitted to the style, or
his means to the conspicuous consumption, of aristocratic
society; his acceptance into the ideological apparatus of the
state, though brilliant for a time, was complicated by his
being, between 1598 and 1610, a Roman Catholic convert.
This was a disadvantageous position, if not an actively
dangerous one in the plot-ridden early years of James I's
reign, and Jonson's motives for adopting it are obscure, but
it seems of a piece with the other determined or chosen
states of relative exile that characterize his career.[28] The self-
advertisement his strategy entailed generated a repertoire of
anecdotes highlighting his pedantry, his uncouth physical
appearance, his irritable pride, his rough humour, and his
immense capacity for drink. This profile modulates, through
the eighteenth and nineteenth centuries, into the myth of
'Ben', the 'difficult' yet estimable and somehow very English
individualist who tramps through the drawing room of the
literary establishment as if he were the head gardener.[29]

What that spectral patronage at once registers and tries to
neutralize is the radical *negativity* of the image of the author.
The freedom to move in and out of literary languages is also
an inability to inhabit any of them: the centre of the competing
verbalizations, where the self-identical author addresses truths
to a god-like posterity, is empty. The word is always the word
of another. At times the writing even appears to emerge from
that absence:

> 'Twere time that I died too, now she is dead,
> Who was my muse, and life of all I said,
> The spirit that I wrote with, and conceived.

All that was good, or great in me she weaved,
And set it forth; the rest were cobwebs fine,
Spun out in name of some of the old nine!
To hang a window, or make dark the room
Till swept away, they were cancelled with a broom!
                    (*Underwoods*, LXXXIV, 9,1–8)

This is not, of course, 'Ben Jonson' unexpectedly confiding in us. It is the opening of the explicitly subtitled 'Apotheosis' of Lady Venetia Digby – that is, the intense tone of depression is the leverage for a massively hyperbolic elegy, fully, if not excessively, an utterance within the code of patronage. But just for that reason the 'she' is transferable, to other patrons, or to the king, or (read against the grain) to the theatre. Without those limiting concretizations, the author is like Face, left in the neglected house with the brooms and spiders, waiting for an alchemist (even a fake one) to put him in words, and fashions.

Which brings us back to Subtle. The fissures in his tirade can be expressed quite simply by asking an actor's question: does Subtle himself believe that he's a real alchemist? If you say that he does, and try to play the lines on that basis, it doesn't work, because the pompous invocations of 'the philosopher's work' are constantly being cut by acknowledgments of the real situation – the borrowed house, the card-sharping and coney-catching. So you can try doing it as if he knows he's a con-man, and is employing alchemical metaphors with a sort of witty aptness: that doesn't work either, because the sheer volume of what you're trying to make the 'vehicle' swamps the tenor; besides, the furious, self-justifying tone of the rhetoric is all wrong for bringing out a string of delicate and recherché in-jokes. This unresolved tension charges individual words with explosive polysemy. 'More than ordinary fellowships', to take one particularly entangled instance, means, at street level, 'better society than you'd meet in the pub'; but 'fellowships' can also mean 'business partnerships' (evoking the Alchemist's pose of being involved in vast financial ventures) *and* 'associations of the faithful' (evoking the play's sustained and scandalous habit of equating alchemy and Puritanism); and then for that last sense 'more than ordinary' slips its commonplace reference and joins the other images, running through the speech, of mundane things divinely exalted. In the neighbourhood of this semantic epicentre, 'fit', 'oaths', 'rules', 'gallant tincture' all shatter in the same fashion; and the disorganizing momentum culminates in that inescapable Jacobean conundrum, 'art'. (Insofar as it means, not Prospero's kind of art, but deception, 'great' loses its air of nobility and just says that Subtle tells *very big* lies.) It starts to look as if it will be difficult to find a sign anywhere in the speech that is still in one piece. The intention of the word, the ray of light, in Bakhtin's metaphor, which it directs at its object, is subject to 'spectral dispersion in an atmosphere filled with the alien words, value judgements and accents through which the ray passes on its way toward the object; the social atmosphere of the word, the atmosphere that surrounds the object, makes the facets of the image sparkle.'[30]

It's true that if we abandon the actor to his difficulties for a moment and shift to the role of readers of literature, an organizing principle does suggest itself. The conjunction of high and low style, or of the aspiring language in which alchemy is real and the reductive language in which it's a swindle, is the kind of pointedly comic juxtaposition we expect to find in ironic-derogatory rhetoric. The play of dialogization is then contained by the horizons of a genre: satire. In certain specialized rhetorical forms, as Bakhtin notes, there is a limited kind of double-voicing which is, however, not really exposed to the 'social atmosphere' of heteroglossia, but remains at most 'merely a distanced echo of this becoming, narrowed down to an individual polemic'.[31] That would be to say: there is after all a dominative unitary language in which the jarring elements of Subtle's utterance 'make sense', but this language is not spoken on the stage – it is that of the author.

But then Subtle, just like Macro, resists his own reduction
to the condition of a satirist's transitory straw man. He resists
it by being a dramatis persona: the continuity of his actions
from one scene to the next sets up the expectation of some
kind of homogeneity in what he says; his words are determined, along lines which cut across those of the authorial
satire, by his relationships with the other people in the story
(thus, he is trying to intimidate Face with the prestige of his
'art', but is also obliged to keep in view the less imaginary
benefits of their partnership); quite a lot of the things he says
are given in the pseudo-real of the drama as *true*. So the play
puts the satiric word into a *situation* – a context which consists,
not only of other words, but of all the things we 'know' about
the people and their circumstances. The polemical intention,
if that really is the origin of the stylistic doubleness, outruns
itself in the form it takes on: Jonson can drive Subtle mad
but not make him go away. The dramatic word and the
authorial word constitute the atmospheric conditions for the
spectral dispersion of each other.

There is, however, an ironic rider to this destabilizing
incursion of authorial negativity into the spectacle. The version of dialogism which I have argued to be characteristic of
Jonson is not, after all, exactly what Bakhtin had in mind.
What he's mainly talking about is the novel, which encom-
passes the 'interanimation of languages' through the simultaneous deployment in a text of a speaker and of a narrator
who is *representing* what the speaker says. It's obvious that
authorial discourse in that sense doesn't occur in drama. (The
author can devise dramatis personae who function as his
spokesmen, and we shall see that Jonson, for reasons which
should be clear enough by now, does this with unflagging
ingenuity. But for these purposes that isn't the same thing.)
How then can authorial discourse be positively staged, rather
than merely emanating stylistic and semantic disturbance
from the wings?

The answer is that what is visibly representing the speech
of another in the theatre is *the actor's performance*. At the heart

of mimetic acting there is, not a simplex gesture, but a dialogue, of extraordinary elasticity, between the representer and the represented, the speaking and the script. How the theatre, or the theatre writer, makes use of this division varies enormously. Jonson uses it as the chink through which authorial discourse gains access to the stage. Putting it like that makes Jonson sound like a Jacobean exponent of *Verfremdung*.[32] That's valid in the limited sense that it would probably be very difficult to identify the whole phenomenon if our own theatre had not been re-aligned by Brecht's decisive gesture of 'literarization'.[33] But the substantive similarities between the two playwrights don't amount to much, nor is there any reason why they should. For the distancing of the actor from the role is not an ingenious supplement to a naturally given acting style in which the two are seamlessly merged. Quite the reverse: that seamlessness is the end product of an extremely complicated technique whose whole purpose is to cover up any trace of such a distance. Ceaseless vigilance is required to prevent the dialogue between the representer and the represented from being overheard by the audience. At lower levels of acting – when a pupil does an impression of the teacher, for instance, or when an actor sends up a colleague in rehearsal – it's exactly the separate co-existence of represented speech and authorial comment, as marked by exaggeration, estranging discontinuity, wilful misrepresentation, and so on, that has the air of naturalness.

For such a style, the monstrosity of Subtle's speech is not just a problem of intelligibility (though it's that too); it's also, itself, an object which can be represented – by marking its items with an over-repetitive gesture, by a pantomime of running out of breath, by abrupt switches between blustering and wheedling, by exaggerating the public tone that's cued by Subtle's oblivious shift into the second person plural at the end. The repertoire of distancing devices is open-ended and constantly changing. Think for example of a current one, which might be called the wounded stare. Identified with Frankie Howerd, but no doubt part of a more extended

tradition, it consists of breaking off and regarding the spectators with a belligerent but pained expression as if defying
them to laugh. It is the feeble gesture of a man who is half-
aware that he has just said something ridiculous or indecent,
and who is trying to outface the dawning realization. But
punctuating that floundering social panic there is, as the
audience knows very well, the conscious timing of a performer
who is using it to get two laughs for the price of one. How
to inflect that duality, where to move next in the ambivalent
fields it sets up, is a matter of very delicate judgement from
one second to the next. Of course, the 'languages' which
intersect in most actual uses of such a device are fairly crude,
operating on quite abstract and ideological paradigms such
as mastery and weakness, norm and violation, and so on. But
the terms of the negotiation between dramatic and authorial
voices are not crude at all, and suggest what resources are
available to the actor for advertising the author's presence
and orchestrating the arguments between his knowledge and
Subtle's life.

Thus Jonson's writing, precisely by the urgency with which
it strains to go beyond the theatre, ends up centred upon the
actor, who finds himself both pushed and required by it. His
word is theatrical in the sense that only on the stage are its
internal contradictions able to gell in the utterance of a
single voice. On the stage, the serried incompatibilities of his
historical engagement with language are reproduced as comic
energy, as laughter.

2 Characters

To abstract from the conclusion of chapter 1: the theatrical word is the site of a fraught conversation between three speakers – the writer, the dramatis persona and the actor. Although these three sources may converge on the moment when a line is actually spoken upon a stage, they remain separable because each has its own orientation: the writer is addressing himself to a reader, the dramatis persona to another dramatis persona, and the actor to an audience. This triad is of course not peculiar to Jonson – it's a general condition of drama in performance. But his theatre produces the structure with peculiar, conflictual sharpness.

It's worth noticing, while considering the model in these general terms, that the unity formed by its three elements is by no means a natural or necessary one. Unlike, say, the signifier and the signified in Saussure's model of the sign, they can be detached from one another not only in theoretical analysis but also in practice. Thus, if we think of each orientation as a 'line' of communication, it's clear that any one of the lines can without absurdity be removed from the structure. Without the writer–reader line there is improvised theatre; without the persona–persona line there is recital or liturgy; without the actor–audience line there is closet drama. Whether all of these forms can properly be described as 'theatre' is beside the point. What counts is that none of the lines is, in itself, needed for a structured communication of some kind to take place – but that, as a matter of fact, all three usually *are* present in mainstream European theatre. The theatrical word is thus characterized by functional superfluity: there's more to it than there needs to be. Moreover, the structure formed in this way has no inherent hierarchy: since none of the lines is indispensable, none has the capacity to enclose or determine the others. They don't stand in a genetic order, or in the relation of text and commentary, or in that of means and ends. They remain in suspension, unstable; the working relationship between them has to be re-established for each occasion.

But then this adjustment is not simply a question of the whims of practitioners. They have options, certainly. To take a well-known example, when Brecht arranged for scenes in his plays to be performed in front of large captions describing what was happening, he was trying to ensure that the persona–persona line was subordinated to the writer–reader line. If these scenes are performed without such a device, the internal composition of the words which are spoken is changed. But choices of this kind are constrained, and their significance determined, by the expectations of the audience, the general conditions of cultural production, the social constitution of the theatre, and, in most societies, the steps taken by the state to control so unreliable a discursive practice.[1] That is what makes the conversation fraught.

In monitoring it, both here and in the previous chapter, I have consistently talked about 'dramatis personae'. This was a necessary awkwardness, because the obvious word – 'character' – is not available for innocent use as a label on a permanent component of the theatrical word. Rather, it is the name of a historically particular adjustment of the whole unstable structure: an orthodoxy which came to power in the English theatre about two hundred years ago, and began to show serious cracks only in the 1950s. What happened, very roughly speaking, was that the writer–reader line and the persona–persona line entered into an intimate combination to marginalize the actor–audience line. The result was a very powerful stabilization which still, today, needs to be subverted if we are to get a clear view of Jonson's stage.

Jonson wrote for a theatre in which the process of marginalization had just begun. When the actors moved out of the street and the banqueting hall into the purpose-built theatres, they ceased to move in space owned and dominated by the spectators, and instead drew the spectators into an enclosure whose permanent focus was the stage. The audience's loss of presence is registered in a shift of convention: whereas in medieval and Tudor theatre the dramatis personae can see and talk to the spectators, in Elizabethan scripts they ignore them. A Shakespearean soliloquy may possibly be regarded as a speech addressed to the audience, but it doesn't explicitly acknowledge that context. The speaker may equally be communing with himself. Seventeenth-century developments accelerate the social disappearance of the audience: the move into indoor theatres rendered the auditorium at once more exclusive and more shadowy, and the change from a thrust stage to a proscenium removed the actors from the encirclement of the public and placed them against a painted drop which, with increasing specificity, represented the locations in which the dramatis personae were supposed to be. In the second half of the eighteenth century, the last, privileged spectators were banished from the acting area, the stage lights were hidden behind flats, and improved lighting of the space upstage started to make it possible for the performers to move back from the proscenium into the set. As part of the same movement, plays with historically or geographically remote settings began, for the first time, to be designed with authenticity in mind: the gorgeous but recognizably contemporary costumes which had hitherto identified actors *as actors* gave way to imitations of the clothes the persons represented would 'really' wear.[2] The principles thus established in the age of Garrick were developed through the nineteenth century until, by its end, the realist theatre, using historical scholarship, gas lighting and three-dimensional sets, had insisted on the proscenium arch, which could not be penetrated by a move or even a glance, and established behind it a photographic simulacrum of reality.[3] The actor–audience line was suppressed, as the actor disappeared into his role and the audience into darkness. The line couldn't be taken out altogether, of course: it was still necessary for the actors and the audience to be in the same room at the same time – at least until the invention of the cinema, which promptly occurred. But it's significant that the culminating phase of its marginalization – say, 1780 to 1914 – was also the heyday of closet drama, both in literary production and in the reception of classic plays.

Around the close of Garrick's career, at a decisive moment of this long revolution, a notable shift in the usage of the word 'character' becomes conspicuous. In the seventeenth century, the term doesn't move far away from its founding sense – a form of writing. A phrase such as 'the character of Dr Donne' is semantically analogous to (though by no means synonymous with) 'the portrait of Dr Donne' – that is, his character is not part of him, but a quite separate object which represents him. The usage within drama isn't essentially different: the ordinary word for a dramatis persona is 'person', and if the 'person' acquires a 'character', it's because we're told 'what he is' in a speech made by someone else. Shakespeare's occasional use of the word in contexts where it evidently means 'face' is consistent with the same sense: it turns on the metaphorical idea that a person's outward appearance is a representation, reliable or otherwise, of the mind within.[4] The constant meaning (as in the current senses, 'letter of the alphabet' and 'mark distinguishing a botanical species') is that a visible mark intentionally made on a surface denotes something other than itself. In short, a 'character' is a sign.

However, when the object denoted by such a sign is a person in a play, the descriptive speech of another dramatis persona is not the only form the sign can take. The character of Morose, for instance, is given by Clerimont and his page in the first scene of *Epicoene* – but it is also given by Jonson.

The totality of what the person is made to say and do in the course of the play can be regarded as a complicated sign denoting what he is: the dramatist's 'character' of him. But then the person, since of course he has no existence outside the play, is himself no more than what is written for him to say and do in the course of it. 'Person' and 'character' turn out to be coterminous, and there's nothing to stop the words becoming interchangeable. This logic can be seen working itself out through Augustan criticism in the pronouns the word 'character' attracts: in Dryden's discussions of Jonson character is always 'it'; in an exchange of letters about comedy in 1696 Congreve (but not his correspondent, Dennis) starts to make it 'he' or 'she'; in Johnson's edition of Shakespeare in 1765 confusion reigns.[5] Following that edition, a number of essays appear in the 1770s and 80s devoted to the characters of Shakespeare — the best known of these is Morgann's on Falstaff (1777).[6] In these, the attempt to hold the distinction between person and character is abandoned, and the latter term becomes, as it has remained, the ordinary word for a person in a drama.

Character has absorbed into itself the object it was supposed to denote. There is no longer anything other than itself which it is representing; consequently, it can no longer be recognized as a sign. It is still treated as one in the sense that it appears, very insistently, as something made by a writer, full of his moral sensibility and his understanding of the human heart, lending itself as never before to the minute elucidation of its *meaning*. But this writing which is character is not displayed on a visible surface; it is inscribed in the mysterious depths of the person's being. It therefore has the closed particularity of someone you meet, but also the legibility of a book that you open. Being and meaning are united in magical existential fullness – a self-representing, self-explaining world. The magic is noted in a new term for the relation between the writer and what he has written: he has 'created' the character. (This connection confirms the view that the decisive moment in the transformation comes in the

1770s – character is a product of the *Genieperiode*, with its mystique of the creative imagination, the quasi-divine original genius of Homer, Milton, Shakespeare.[7]

Thus the theatrical mechanism which suppresses the actor–audience line, covering up all the signs of the actor's relationship with the theatre (stage, lights, audience, playing time) and surrounding him with the signs of the dramatis persona's relationship with his world (costume, room, acquaintances, fictional time), has as its point the illusory autonomy of the persona–persona line; however, this is achieved, not at the expense of the writer–reader line, but through its apotheosis. The writer, or now more appropriately the author, is present in every word the characters utter, not as the divisive commentator we saw in chapter 1, but as the creator whose wisdom permeates them all, ordering and animating their superficially casual exchanges. It's a Deist universe, whose Maker expresses himself only through his creatures. Direct revelation of his intentions is prohibited by the principle of regularity which guarantees the creatures' autonomy and consequently his own divinity, and whose name is Nature. And just as the effect of Jonson's denaturing interventions was to give to the actor–audience line the dynamic emphasis of comic estrangement, so the integrity of Nature requires that the actor–audience line, the actuality of the *show*, should be as weak as possible.

It's therefore not surprising that the beginning of the sovereignty of character is marked by the end of Jonson's viability on the stage. Six of his plays were revived after the theatres re-opened in 1660: of these, *Catiline* ceased to be performed around the end of the century, *Bartholomew Fair* dropped out of the repertoire in the 1730s, and three – *The Alchemist*, *Epicoene* and *Volpone* – all disappeared during the decade or so following Garrick's retirement in 1776. *Every Man In His Humour* was revived, in a somewhat antiquarian spirit, three or four times in the nineteenth century, the last time in 1838.[8] With that isolated and partial exception, the stage history of Jonson in the theatre of illusion is a blank. His drama is, so to speak, something the self-representing character has in its past, which it lives by forgetting.

This is ironic, because within the Elizabethan theatre it was Jonson who put himself forward as the pioneering exponent of the natural, in rather pointed contrast with Shakespeare: 'He [that is, Jonson himself] is loth to make Nature afraid in his plays, like those that beget Tales, Tempests, and such like drolleries' (*Bartholomew Fair*, Induction, 113–15). What is more, this project explicitly entails an attempt to subordinate the actor–audience line to the speech of the writer. The *Bartholomew Fair* Induction as a whole is a serio-comic presentation of a 'contract' defining the proper relationship between the audience and the poet, going over the heads, as it were, of the actors. And the first audience of *The Staple of News* was welcomed with this rather discouraging announcement:

> For your own sakes, not his, he bade me say,
> Would you were come to hear, not see a play.
> Though we his actors must provide for those,
> Who are our guests, here, in the way of shows,
> The maker hath not so.
>
> (Prologue, 1–5)

The desire to insulate the play from the actuality of the show could hardly be more graphically expressed. Though, as we shall see, the difference between the desire and the fact is in this case crucial, it's nonetheless clear that Jonson regards the relationship between actor and audience as a threat to the success of his naturalistic innovations.

The issues are most forcefully set out in the prologue to *Every Man In His Humour*. This text, with its crisp air of saying exactly what Jonson means, is already a rather overburdened workhorse in the interpretation of the plays, but it's unavoidable. It tells the public that the poet

                                    hath not so loved the stage,
As he dare serve the ill customs of the age: ...
To make a child, now swaddled, to proceed
Man, and then shoot up, in one beard and weed,
Past threescore years: or, with three rusty swords,
And help of some few foot-and-half-foot words,
Fight over York and Lancaster's long jars:
And in the tiring-house bring wounds to scars.
He rather prays you will be pleased to see
One such, today, as other plays should be.
Where neither Chorus wafts you o'er the seas;
Nor creaking throne comes down, the boys to please;
Nor nimble squib is seen, to make afeard
The gentlewomen; nor rolled bullet heard
To say it thunders; nor tempestuous drum
Rumbles, to tell you when the storm doth come;
But deeds, and language, such as men do use:
And persons, such as Comedy would choose,
When she would show an image of the times
And sport with human follies, not with crimes.

                           (Prologue, 3–24)[9]

Rather surprisingly for the prologue to a play, this devotes
almost all of its extremely detailed references to the theatre
to a description of the kind of performance the spectators are
not about to see. When it gets to its eventual 'but', it holds
the logical antithesis for only one line before moving incon-
sequentially on to a discussion of the moral scope of comedy
as a genre. The effect of this assymetry is to place the 'ill
customs' and the way plays ought to be in the relation of
marked to unmarked: on the one hand, there is a motley
assortment of laborious representational devices; on the other,
an 'image of the times' which apparently projects itself by no
definite theatrical means at all. The former is marked by two
things, both adroitly stressed to the point of absurdity. One
is the materiality of the stage production – the way its make-
up, costumes, props and speeches remain obstinately them-

selves, refusing to merge, as the sardonically literal verbs ('make', 'shoot up', 'fight over') suggest they're meant to, with the world they represent. The other thing is the production's direct address to the audience: the crude atmospheric devices, it's implied, are only there for the sake of their effect on childish and impressionable spectators. The converse demand is that the actor–audience line should stay out of sight, not deforming with its miscellaneous contingencies the aptness and truth of the 'image of the times'.

If we look at this in the terms of literary history, it's clear that Jonson is identifying himself with the neo-classical tendencies in Renaissance poetics which were institutionalized a little later in the seventeenth century as 'the rules'.[10] The prologue is saturated with references to Horace, Cicero, Aristotle and Sidney, and if its recommendations are abstracted in the form of rules, the result is a fairly complete outline of the neo-classical canon:

1 unity of time, place and action;
2 exclusion from the stage of events which would strain credulity;
3 stable separation of genres;
4 decorum of language;
5 decorum in the portrayal of persons;
6 combination of pleasure and moral instructiveness.

To see how these principles encompass a drama of the 'natural' in opposition to the materiality of the stage, we can look more closely at the one Jonson enlarges upon most – the unity of time. To a modern, empiricist naturalism, the rule that the action should be confined to the space of a single day seems curiously arbitrary. Once two or three hours' playing time have been made to stand for twenty-four, stage time and 'real' time have been decisively identified as not the same; so what conceivable internal principle prevents the play from accommodating a month or a lifetime? The answer is that the limit of a day, although strictly speaking it permits some time to pass, effectively excludes the constituents of *historical* time: repetition and change. Repetition, because a single day implies a single waking, a single dinner time, a single session of the court (so that, insofar as the day is the image of man's life, its images of beginning, conviviality, justice are universal ones); and change, because, as Jonson vividly and negatively points out, the external conditions of a person's existence – his physical state, his clothes, the weather, the country where he is and its government – can be expected in this timescale to remain the same. Thus things and – what matters from our point of view here – people *never have to be shown as differing from themselves*. It's not that nothing is allowed to change; on the contrary, striking reversals and revelations are positively called for by Aristotelian principles of dramatic construction. But the changes must be such that they can be completed within one day; and that means they can always be comprehended by a unified subjectivity, assimilated into the unbroken consciousness which is sustained between one sleep and the next.[11] Once this rule is broken, so is the oneness of 'nature'; splits appear between the conscious and the biological, the word and the truth, the immediate and the historical; the dramatis persona ceases to be self-identical and acquires, as it were, an unconscious. In the theatre, the actuality of the show reasserts itself, as something more or less analogous to the rolled bullet is 'heard/To say', 'Some days later ....'

It's easy enough to see how each of the other rules operates in parallel fashion to ward off other threats to the singleness of dramatic consciousness. Taken all together (the unity of time is obviously not a *sufficient* condition of the 'natural'), they legislate to confine the theatrical representation within a unitary language that underwrites the self-identity of the dramatis personae – that is, to proscribe the latent dialogism of theatre. In this function, the 'unities' declare themselves as the ancestor of 'character', or, better, the matrix in which it was formed. For although by the 1770s the neo-classical canon has taken on the aspect of a formalistic 'art' against which a newer conception of 'nature' defines itself, the former's legal settlement of a *single* reality, one devoid of the self-divisions and incompletenesses of historical becoming, makes essentially the same closure as the quasi-spontaneous fusion of language and being which constitutes character. An admirer of Shakespeare wrote in 1775 that 'however he may sport, as he often does, with the three unities of Aristotle, time, place and action, he seldom sins against a fourth, which I am surprised the Critics have not added, as being worth them all – namely, that of *character*.'[12]

The substitution this all but proposes is possible because of the underlying homology of the two kinds of unity. On the other hand, it's desirable because the Aristotelian, or rather neo-Aristotelian, unities have obvious weaknesses. They exclude those potentialities of language and theatre which would introduce difference into the dramatis personae by what is really an arbitrary decree. However dominant the rules became in a particular aesthetic ideology, they could never create a situation in which it was hard to imagine a play that violated them – on the contrary, extended times-cales, onstage murders, tragicomedies and the rest press against them the more insistently for being repeatedly alluded to as things one mustn't do. With the establishment of charac-ter, on the other hand, the text of the law is written on the person of the drama, absolutely constitutive of his interiority. The rules can be relinquished because the unity they police has become inevitable; and not only relinquished, but mili-tantly rejected, because once the unity of the dramatic subject is assured, they appear as fetters on its free development.

Although Jonson broke most of his rules at some time or other, he certainly took them much more seriously than any of his English contemporaries, keeping to them most of the time, and occasionally appending theoretical defences of transgressions.[13] This is in itself a reason for his absence from the nineteenth-century stage: necessarily blind to the authoritarian basis of its own spontaneity, the theatre of character found the restraints imposed by Jonson on the freedom of action and the self-expression of his dramatis personae unintelligible and pedantic. If he was the father of 'natural' comedy, he was its heavy father.

But then that mythical way of putting it starts to suggest a primal innocence on which the law of unity supervened around the end of the sixteenth century. This won't do: medieval and Tudor theatre can't really be seen as a carefree celebration of the multiplicity of the signifier. Or rather, it can be seen like that for certain purposes – Bill Bryden's work with the Mystery Cycles (National Theatre, 1977–85) discovered them, precisely, as a means of liberating text, objects, actors and audience from the representational rigidities of naturalism – but only by adopting a somewhat narrowly aesthetic point of view. For as Glynne Wickham has shown, the Elizabethan theatre's non-illusionist inheritance was an *emblematic* stage – that is, one in which an extreme disunity of dramatic consciousness was controlled by a deliberate and stable distinction between 'earnest' and 'game'.[14] Practically anything, technically speaking, could be shown – the passage of forty days with Noah inside the ark, the crucifixion of Christ, the birth and death of mankind, the direct utterances of God. The distances involved between representation and object dwarf Jonson's anxieties about the Wars of the Roses. But that's not a real contrast, because the emblematic performance isn't properly speaking a representation at all. It's a game, something like a festival observance, commemorating or celebrating, in a local and specific manner, universal events. In other words, the terms of the dramatic showing are not in the last analysis mimetic, but sacramental. The problem of timescales doesn't arise, because the plane of the 'earnest' is eternal. The actuality of the show doesn't compromise the self-identity of the dramatis personae, because it's impossible, anyway, to conceive of a person as self-representing – that is, as a subject abstracted from the objective discourse of death, judgement, heaven and hell. It was the destruction of this radically unified stage in the course of the Reformation which posed the question of 'natural' representation in the first place.

Despite that break-up, very significant sections of the emblematic vocabulary were still in living use in Elizabethan theatre; in masques and civic pageants, but also as structural elements in new plays, including some of Jonson's own.[15] But his drama as a whole places itself in opposition to that inheritance, not only in prologues and inductions, but also in the extraordinary critical structure of his last major comedy, *The Devil Is An Ass*.

The nub of the plot is a satirist's conceit: a devil visits contemporary London intending to work mischief, and finds himself outclassed by the mischief which is being carried on without his assistance. But the play combines that theme with a reflection on the theatre itself, because it presents its infernal characters in a parody of morality drama. Satan, who enters with a traditional roar, selects the play's main human figure, Fitzdottrel, as a man ripe for damnation, and sends a junior devil, Pug, to offer himself as his servant. At the end of his role, Pug exits with Iniquity, whose dagger and long coat, and farcical doggerel couplets, identify him as a reconstruction of the Vice of the Tudor interludes. Pug's journey from hell to London is thus an interstylistic one: he enters the new theatre, the 'image of the times', as an emissary from the old. He does so on the new theatre's terms: he is in London for one day only, and not in an 'airy' manifestation, but in an existing human body (made available by a hanging at Tyburn) in which he is 'subject / To all impression of the flesh' (I.i.134–8). His cosmic identity, thus confined within the rules of a human one, immediately starts to get confused. Fitzdottrel is not Everyman, but a socially particularized fool who has, among other manias, a frivolous interest in the occult. Mistaking this for a serious allegiance, Pug introduces himself as a real devil, called Devil; Fitzdottrel doesn't believe him, but accepts him as a servant, whimsically, for the sake of his name. Instead of making sense as a term in an eschatological language which defines the human, the devil is himself defined by an idiosyncratic human language which makes him into a joke.

This ironic humanism deepens when Pug gets involved in the play's first main event, the attempted seduction by Wittipol of Fitzdottrel's wife. Recognizing this project as the kind of thing he ought to promote, Pug energetically urges her to cuckold her husband. This tempting is so blatant that Mrs Fitzdottrel assumes it's a trick: 'This can be / None but my husband's wit ... It creaks his Engine' (II.ii.85–7). That is, not having access to the metaphysical reason for Pug's immoralism, she has recourse to a psychological explanation – her husband's fatuous belief in his own cunning. As a matter of fact, she *is* quite interested in the idea of cuckolding him, so to protect her position she complains to him about Pug's behaviour. Pug is punished, and when Mrs Fitzdottrel secretly meets Wittipol, revenges himself on her by betraying the assignation to Fitzdottrel. There's a double irony in this development. Firstly, Pug has been instrumental in *preventing* an act of adultery: in his spontaneous attempt at malice he has, so to speak, forgotten which side he's meant to be on. But secondly, Wittipol's lovemaking is conducted at such a pitch of sensuous wit, and Fitzdottrel's interruption is such a crass combination of violence and self-pity, that it's impossible to avoid the sense that the illicit relationship is on a higher moral plane than the marriage. The terms in which such a judgement can be articulated are clearly outside the vocabulary of the emblematic stage: among them is 'character'. A drama of individual particularity defines itself in the process of burlesquing a drama of theological values.

Yet the road from Jonson to the theatre of character is not exactly open. For what this account has played down is that Pug's clueless handling of the 'human' world is above all due to his inability to cope with *illusion*. The people he meets never say what they mean. He tells Fitzdottrel the truth and is not believed. He gives Mrs Fitzdottrel his true opinion and she concludes that he's playing a double game; moreover, she *is* playing a double game, not only in her tactical complaint about him, but also in the message she sends through him to Wittipol, which appears to be a proper wifely dismissal but is actually a coded encouragement. (Wittipol decodes it correctly; Pug is fooled.) Meanwhile, in the main property plot, Fitzdottrel is being swindled by a con-man who offers him delusive visions of being a millionaire duke; the con-man is eventually outmanoeuvred by Wittipol in disguise. By the end of the play, Fitzdottrel is desperately trying to escape his financial entanglements by pretending to be possessed by the devil; only the revelation, after the twenty-four hours are up, that Pug really was a devil shames him into abandoning his fits. The 'natural' reason why the devil is an ass is inverted: it's not that the new theatre presents a real world in which the visitor from the old one is exposed as an extravagant fiction, but that the visitor is real and for that very reason helpless among the layers of false appearance which make up the image of the times. Jonson has dramatized the passage from emblem to image, from the theatre of religious allegory to the secular theatre of illusion. But the latter is denaturalized by its constant teasing consciousness of, precisely, illusion.

This is not only because the coherence of the represented world is fissured by the differences generated by the intrigue. The stylistic juxtaposition itself is equally disruptive: the devil device, while very broadly parodying the moralities, also estranges the image of the modern city. And that strangeness is compounded by the surprising way the play, despite observing the unities of time and place (hell aside), registers, at the level of imagery, the passing of historical time. It affects hell: the Vice is clearly senile, and Satan, sounding like the despondent owner of a declining family business, explains to him testily that his naive folk-devilry has been rendered obsolete by newer metropolitan fashions in vice. He thinks Pug might stand a chance in Lancashire or Northumberland, but as for London, one must remember that this is 1616, not 1560 (I.i.23–130). The exactness of the dates and places, hinting at the link between the emblematic theatre and Catholicism, introduces into the script a relativizing awareness of the historical conditions of its own conventions. At a different level of the text, the con-man has a speech, 'in the character' of the wealthy property speculator he is only pretending to be, in celebration of the slow rhythms by which the securest estates pass out of the hands of their owners into those of lawyers and projectors:

Nature hath these vicissitudes. She makes
No man a state of perpetuity, sir.
(II.iv.38–9)

This is not the 'nature' of the stage: the language reaches out beyond the comic day towards determinants it can't accommodate. But the strongest image of this unstageable time is wittily theatrical. Wittipol makes his first addresses to Mrs Fitzdottrel by giving her husband an expensive cloak in return for his permission to talk to her, in the husband's presence but uninterrupted, for a quarter of an hour. The complex scene which results sets Wittipol's eloquent *carpe diem* –

Flowers,
Though fair, are oft but of one morning. Think,
All beauty doth not last until the autumn.
You grow old, while I tell you this.
(I.vi.128–31)

– against Fitzdottrel, sitting silenced with his eyes on his watch, gloating over the passing of the minutes which will secure him the cloak. The effect is to make real evanescence – the time in which the actors and the audience are living – a motive force in the scene: the fictive 'unity of time' is exploded from within. A baroque ornament to the scene confirms the point. The transaction takes place in the morning; Fitzdottrel is intending to go to the theatre in the afternoon and take a seat on the stage to show off his new cloak. The play he is going to see is called *The Devil Is An Ass*.

This incursion of open time into the closed time of the dramatic form dislocates the characters too. Thus, the logic which is generated by its penetration of the wooing scenes clearly includes the destruction of the Fitzdottrel marriage. But such an event couldn't possibly be accommodated either within the one day or within the comic decorum which excludes serious violations of the law. So in a later scene (IV.vi) Mrs Fitzdottrel explains that she was only ever looking for a friend who could help her to cope with the consequences of her husband's folly. The emerging love affair which had appeared, in the first two acts, to be the directly 'human' bottom line to the elaborate negotiations of parody and deception, turns out to have been, itself, a further kind of play-acting. This is, as the theatre of character says, 'not convincing' – that is, it spoils our sense of Mrs Fitzdottrel as a person who is present and legible at the same time, and introduces into the representation of her relations with Wittipol an *argument* between desire and prudence, transgressive and conformable love, which is not natural but estrangingly discursive.

As at the level of dramatic speech, then, the immediately divisive factor, setting the contradictions of the 'times' against the self-consistency of the 'image', is the insistence of the authorial discourse. As the *Every Man In* prologue made clear, with its sharp opposition between the poet and the stage, the condition of the neo-classical canon is for Jonson above all the monologic predominance of the writer–reader line. The play aspires to be what another preface calls a 'legitimate poem' (*Catiline*, dedication), whose rhetorical purposes are simply served by the illustrative exchanges of the dramatis personae and the secondary interpretations of the actors. But since Jonson has, historically, no access to the myth of creativity which would naturalize such a hierarchy of the theatrical word, the resulting organization of the spectacle is essentially polemical. The prologue ends by hoping that the spectators, 'that have so graced monsters, may like men'; but the men are so traversed and anatomized by the text which produces them that their appearance becomes monstrous after all.

Monsters formed an indispensable category in the neo-classical canons of representation I've been discussing.

As conceived by these canons, the body was first of all
a strictly completed, finished product. Furthermore, it
was isolated, alone, fenced off from all other bodies.
All signs of its unfinished character, of its growth and
proliferation were eliminated; its protuberances and off-
shoots were removed, its convexities (signs of new
sprouts and buds) smoothed out, its apertures closed ...
The accent was placed on the completed, self-sufficient
individuality of the given body.[16]

This is a precise visual translation of that single nature which
in the theatre is projected by the unities. Monstrosity is
the proscribed other of that self-sufficient individuality, the
suppressed and hideous physiognomy of incompleteness and
difference. Jonson was conscious of the visual parallel: in
Discoveries he notes a passage in Vitruvius 'where he complains
of their painting chimeras, by the vulgar unaptly called gro-
tesques: saying, that men who were truly born to study,
and emulate nature, did nothing but make monsters against
nature; which Horace so laughed at' (1938–43). The chimera
– a fantastic creature combining human and animal features
– is the definitive type of monster: a direct affront to the
single and self-contained body. Its *locus classicus*, the human-
headed horse at the very opening of the *Ars Poetica*, is probably
what Jonson is referring to in the *Every Man In* prologue. As
one would expect, Jonson's theatre excludes chimeras –
though the 'tortoise' episode in *Volpone* is enough to show that
the image was available to him. But a related monstrosity
provides his best known principle of 'characterization':

Cob   Nay, I have my rheum, and I can be angry as well
        as another, sir.
Cash Thy rheum, Cob? Thy humour, thy humour? Thou
        mistakst.
Cob   Humour? Mack, I think it be so, indeed: what is that
        humour? Some rare thing, I warrant.
Cash Marry, I'll tell thee, Cob: it is a gentleman-like
        monster, bred in the special gallantry of our time
        by affectation; and fed by folly.
                    (*Every Man In His Humour*, III.iv.12–20)

The pseudo-natural history is typical: a monster is usually identified by its unnatural generation and sustenance, again drawing attention to its compound, non-self-identical quality.

A humour, as Jonson adroitly recalls through Cob's creative malapropism, is literally a body fluid. It's part of the medical representation of the 'fenced off' classical body, in that the starting point of Hippocratic anatomy was a distinction between those parts of the body which are containing (organs, veins, skin, etc.) and those which are contained (blood, juices, spirits). It's this need to be contained which is the decisive characteristic for Asper, who defines the idea with scholastic formality in the Induction to *Every Man Out Of His Humour*: he states that anything which combines the properties of moisture and fluxure, 'As wanting power to contain itself' (97), is humour, and only then goes on to say that

> choler, melancholy, phlegm, and blood,
> By reason that they flow continually
> In some one part, and are not continent,
> Receive the name of humours.
> (Induction, 99–102)

Health is the condition in which these various flows are contained and co-ordinated in a single system under the governance of the heart, 'the seat and fountain of life, ... the sun of our body, the king and sole commander of it'.[17] To the extent that this happens, the state of the individual's body and mind approximates to a norm, which is not much use for the differentiation of dramatis personae. The *comedy* of humours is produced when the incontinence manifests itself in the arbitrary predominance of one of them, a systemic disorder which gives rise to temperamental bias in moderate cases, and extremely to disease and madness. To the extent that this happens – and consequently that the typing serves to distinguish dramatis personae from one another – the humorous individual becomes a monster, because the flow of humour is governing the affections of the heart, which is an inversion of the natural hierarchy, and because the over-running of the stable distinction between containing and contained produces uncontrolled appetites and discharges (the 'feeding' and 'venting' of humour) which compromise the integrity and self-sufficiency of the body. Although Jonson uses the medical terminology in a quite freely metaphorical sense, that imagery of physical anomie comes powerfully through into the plays. Kitely's jealousy in *Every Man In*

> as a subtle vapour, spreads itself
> Confusedly through every sensive part,
> Till not a thought, or motion, in the mind,
> Be free from the black poison of suspect.
>
> (II.iii.64–7)

Crites, the *raisonneur* of *Cynthia's Revels*, denounces the court humorist whose

> best and understanding part,
> (The crown and strength of all his faculties)
> Floats like a dead drowned body, on the stream
> Of vulgar humour, mixed with common'st dregs.
>
> (I.v.33–6)

And Caesar in *Poetaster* praises those who rule their lives by knowledge

> and can becalm
> All sea of humour, with the marble trident
> Of their strong spirits.
>
> (IV.vi.74–6)

What is also striking, and typical, in these formulations is their political content. The image of humour as a monstrous absence of form projects a counter-image of the mind as an absolute monarch, the sole source of value and order. In this sense, humours comedy appears as a logical development of neo-classical dramaturgy in general, producing in physical and psychological terms the juridical, arbitrary power which, as opposed to any kind of self-sustaining organism, *decrees* the unity and viability of individual consciousness. This absolutist duality of monarchy and anarchy appears not only within the microcosm (the humorous individual as an ungovernable state), but also in the humorist's relationship with the society of the play. For as Cash hints in the exchange I began by quoting, 'humour' is not only a term in medicine – it's also a social craze, a piece of the neurotic exhibitionism known as gallantry which was associated with the unprecedented mobility of landed power and its attendant crisis of status in the 1580s and 90s.[18] In the fashionable, 'gentlemanly' usage which Jonson is picking up and caricaturing, the point of the word is that it's almost entirely meaningless. Sogliardo, for instance, the rustic social climber in *Every Man Out Of His Humour*, uses it all the time as a sort of elementary badge of gentlemanly status. In one exchange he is caught out in a somewhat ungentlemanly enthusiasm for hobby-horse dancing (a peasant amusement):

Sogliardo ... I have danced in it myself too.
Carlo   Not since the humour of gentility was upon you? Did you?
Sogliardo Yes, once; marry, that was but to show what a gentleman might do, in a humour.
Carlo   Oh, very good.
Mitis   Why, this fellow's discourse were nothing, but for the word humour.
Cordatus Oh, bear with him; and he should lack matter, and words too, 'twere pitiful.

(II.i.44–53)

This is monstrous in a rather different sense: the *word* is a monster because it's a conversational something begotten by a semantic nothing. Asper, in the Induction (109–14), has tried to make a clear distinction between this kind of vacuous use and the word's legitimate sense; but in practice the distinction doesn't hold, because even properly speaking, the amorphousness of humour makes it unintelligible as such, a discursive negation. Humorous behaviour is action which

is accountable to no reasoned ethical scheme whatever: to
questions about its purpose and justification it replies with
Shylock's circularity, 'It is my humour'. This answer marks
the no-go area of discursive order; it is individual difference
conceived of as absolutely anti-social, the meaningless retort
of the incontinent fluxure to the containing structure. The
'gallant' use of the word to express an empty individualism
is thus quite consistent with its function as a device for
organizing persona. Take, for instance, the moment in *Every
Man In* when Stephen, the 'country gull' who has adopted
melancholy as his humour, meets a kindred spirit in Matthew,
the town gull:

Matthew	I am melancholy myself divers times, sir, and then do I no more but take pen and paper presently, and overflow you half a score, or a dozen of sonnets, at a sitting.
(Edward Knowell	Sure, he utters them, then, by the gross.)
Stephen	Truly, sir, and I love such things, out of measure.
Edward Knowell	[*Aside*] I'faith, better than in measure, I'll undertake.

(III.i.77–82)

The punning play with the idea of incontinence – 'overflow',
'utter', 'gross', 'measure' – makes the pretentious language of
humour yield meaning after all, in a reductive and scatological
realization of its imagery.

But then that secondary, interpretive speech objectifies
the language of the humorist himself, representing him as
incapable of representing himself. Humour, it seems, is not
able to signify; it comes out only as babble or excrement. It
must be signified by something else. The role of the stage
spectator, the moderator who speaks what the humorist is,
becomes crucial. The presence of such a figure is conspicuous
in all but one of the examples I gave while discussing humour.

Thus despite its potential for differentiating personae, humour is not really a method of characterization. For instead of approaching the union of sign and person which we saw to be constitutive of realist character, the humours model drives them apart, usually presenting them as two separate figures on the stage, and even deriving the dramatic action from the conflict between the two. In other words, stage humours depend for their effect on a deeper structural principle, which is the writing down of a person by another – the *Jacobean* type of character.

'Character' in the narrowest sense was a minor literary genre, deriving from the *Characters* of Theophrastus, which were published in a scholarly edition in the 1590s. It consisted essentially of a terse prose description of a behavioural type, though variants such as professional types and even places were admitted in the course of the form's fairly playful development. It's an offshoot of classical rhetoric, associated with the figure of *descriptio* which plays an important part in the Ciceronian *argumentum ad hominem*, and its rather short-lived popularity reflects the almost total control exercised over pre-university education in the Renaissance by rhetorical categories of invention and style.[19] Consistently with this pedagogic background, its underlying form is intralinguistic: the pure Theophrastan character is an extended definition of a given adjective. For instance: 'Stinginess is a disproportionate avoidance of expense. The stingy man is the sort who will come to your house in the middle of the month and ask you for half a month's interest on his loan. When he is at table ... etc.[20]

It's a technique, that's to say, for assimilating behavioural difference into the generalized discourse of official culture. The aim in writing is to take the apparently random diversity of observable social behaviour and reduce it to classified gestures which, because once noted they can be seen as repetitive, are able to function as signs. The art of it is to select details which are so striking and minute as to seem unconditionally idiosyncratic, but which prove, once they're arranged in the field controlled by the adjective, to be a witty kind of naming. The knowledge which emerges is of the order, not of understanding (there's no interest in *why* a person might be stingy), but of recognition: it's a character in the root sense that it sets down, not an actual or fictional individual who is stingy, but the marks by which the reader may identify stinginess in such cases as he encounters in his life.

The resulting tone often strikes a modern reader as *managerial*. 'A Modest Man' in one of the seventeenth-century collections, for example,

> sees nothing more willingly than his errors; and it is his error sometimes to be too soon persuaded. He is content to be auditor where he only can speak, and content to go away and think himself instructed. No man is so weak that he is ashamed to learn of, and is less ashamed to confess it ...[21]

We aren't invited to imagine being such a person, but to consider what are likely to be the strengths and weaknesses of the way he conducts his affairs, perhaps to use these general reflections to predict what he will do in a particular situation. 'Character' writing survives today in this sense not in literature, but as part of the selection process for jobs and promotions: in that genre too, the point is not to suggest the individual's unique subjectivity, but to predicate her within a ruling discourse of general criteria. It's not a coincidence that charactery flourished during a period when the centralization of state power and the demilitarization of the aristocracy were obliging the ruling class to acquire (in the first instance through a training in rhetoric) bureaucratic skills.[22]

The placing and judging accent of this way of knowing people is made still more insistent by the polemical structure of classical rhetoric, its roots in pleading. As W.J. Ong says, *encomium* and *vituperatio* formed the centre of oratorical expertise: 'Renaissance literary performance in practice and even more in theory hinged on these two activities to a degree quite incredible today.'[23] Most characters belong unambiguously to one class or the other. There's no formal space in which to establish an idea of the person as an independent entity and *then* (as it were) express an opinion about it. Because the immediate object of the discourse is a word, the character is encomiastic or vituperative from the start.

When, consequently, the form is moved out of the artificial autonomy of the character books and on to the stage, what immediately becomes obvious is that to define a person in this way is to exercise power – either the effective power of quasi-bureaucratic assessment, or the aggressive, unconfirmed power of persuasive rhetoric. To 'characterize' a dramatis persona is not to constitute, but to invade, its interiority, to subordinate it to one's own word, to make it thing-like and knowable. Obviously this subordination can never be quite complete so long as its object, as presented by an actor, is there on the stage, visibly something other than the words which nail him. So the struggle of the discourse to dominate the persons can become a dramatic conflict in itself. In fact, in the experimental 'comical satires' of 1599–1601, where Jonson abandons conventional comic plotting, it's virtually the only dramatic action.

In *Every Man Out Of His Humour*, for example, it is organized on two levels, the persons of the play proper, who characterize one another, and two stage spectators, Cordatus and Mitis, who discuss what they see between and even during the scenes. For the reader there is also a third level, because Jonson appends prose characters of everybody to the cast list in the published script. The most articulate figures within the play are Carlo Buffone and Macilente; they are given by the authorial characters – sketched in their names, which are also characterizing ones – as a 'public, scurrilous and profane jester', who scrounges dinners on the strength of his scandalous table talk, and an envious scholar. Both clever talkers, they co-operate for much of the play in expounding and persecuting its fools, but they also deliver vicious characters of each other. Macilente's Buffone is

> an open-throated, black-mouthed cur,
> That bites at all, but eats on those that feed him.
> A slave, that to your face will, serpent-like,
> Creep on the ground, as he would eat the dust;
> And to your back will turn the tail, and sting
> More deadly than a scorpion.
>
> (I.ii.202–7)

This is more hostile than the version offered by Cordatus, but it recognizably works on the same 'marks': 'an impudent common jester, a violent railer, and an incomprehensible epicure; one whose company is desired of all men, but beloved of none; he will sooner lose his soul than a jest, and profane even the most holy things to excite laughter ...' (Induction 336–41). In a sense the gap in tone between these two characters is the measure of Macilente's malice; certainly Buffone's character of him seeks to take the authority out of his condemnations by making them into signs of what *Macilente* is, rather than of those he attacks: 'he looks as if he were chap-fallen with barking at other men's good fortunes: 'ware how you offend him; he carries oil and fire in his pen, will scald where it drops: his spirit's like powder, quick, violent: he'll blow a man up with a jest ...' (I.ii.184–8). But although that challenges the power of Macilente's character of Buffone by counter-characterizing it, it doesn't invalidate it: apart from anything else, its delivery, in an aside, to a third person whom Buffone has told Macilente he despises, furnishes an example of the kind of social opportunism Macilente is talking about. The play's two internal satirists, the jester and the scholar, remain in contention, neither having established power over the other.

Since Cordatus is a friend of Asper, who has written the play that Buffone is in, his character may be regarded as having some authority. But in a further twist, Buffone provides a character of the author himself as a pot-poet, sponging on the conviviality of the actors (Induction, 318–29). This involvement of the poet in the game of character is a *jeu d'esprit*, but an appropriate one; for this mode of reifying aggression is also that of the play itself in its handling of the dramatis personae. The action of 'putting them out of their humours' is a series of violent exposures conspicuously engineered by the author (the function of the two stage spectators is partly to draw attention to just this intervention). The uxorious husband is brought to the sight of his wife kissing a courtier; the courtier is arrested for debt; the social hanger-on is left with the bill for a party at which Buffone has had his scurrilous mouth sealed with wax; and so on. Each one is anatomized by the imperious articulations of the text, and each, once he has been fixed in an attitude which simultaneously characterizes and punishes him, vanishes, his role concluded.

Asper, the author, has said in the Induction that his language

> Was never ground into such oily colours,
> To flatter vice and daub iniquity:
> But with an armed and resolved hand,
> I'll strip the ragged follies of the time
> Naked, as at their birth

Cordatus   Be not too bold,
Asper   You trouble me – and with a whip of steel,
> Print wounding lashes in their iron ribs.

(14–20)

The contrast between paint and print is exact: the mineral not ground down for pigment to create illusions, but sharpened for use as a tool to engrave characters. The violence of the latter image, the incisive anti-physis of writing, is luridly brought out: Asper is proposing a theatre in which, as in Kafka's penal settlement, the judicial text is inscribed on the bodies of the malefactors.[24] 'Character' has become the principle of construction for a whole play, and the principle turns out to be sadistic.

However, as is obvious from the sheer oddity of the play

as I have described it, the mechanism also resembles Kafka's in failing to produce the authoritative text it's supposed to. Instead of the manifestation of justice which is promised by the memory of the classical past, we see a performance marked by dilapidation, cruelty, monstrosity. The controlling author, Asper, is out of control. This is signalled by the debunking little interruption by Cordatus at the climax of the Juvenalian tirade quoted above, and also in Asper's curious relations with his fiction: he himself takes, and vanishes into, the role of Macilente, who is the principal dramatic agent of the exposures and punishments, and whose pathological envy therefore appears as a parodic version of Asper's incorruptible commitment to truth. The whole characterizing intention is thus itself decomposed by writing, reduced to a humour. The formal coherence of the text is correspondingly undermined, as the fantastic estrangements of the play-within-a-play device pull every potential *locus standi* into doubleness and self-parody. Jonson on Asper on Macilente on Buffone on Sogliardo ... signification itself is all but dissipated in the proliferation of authors.

It's a crisis of authority. As we have seen, the dramatic unities, the concept of humour as incontinent fluidity, and the domination of individual difference by writing, are all predicated within the syntax of arbitrary power, with its structural opposition of singleness (as order) and plurality (as anarchy). That's to say: in these plays the dramatis persona is problematized within the ideology of absolutism. Consequently, the only sign which appears as really identical with itself, and so able to arrest the decomposing process of character and parody, is literally the monarch, the formal source of power and value, who is also a real person. This is the solution adopted by Jonson in all three comical satires: in *Cynthia's Revels* the authority of the poet figure Crites is validated by Cynthia, the queen of the court and an allegorical representation of Elizabeth; in *Poetaster* the victory of Horace over the false poets is guaranteed in exactly the same way by Caesar; and in *Every Man Out* itself the play ends, after all the others have been put out of their humour, with Macilente being magically relieved of his black envy by the sunlight of the Queen's presence – this resolution was devised for the court performance, but Jonson seems to have tried to use it, controversially, in the public theatre too by having Elizabeth represented by an actor.[25]

In this very particular case, the unity of nature is restored, and the monsters banished, by an externally given principle analogous to the theologically given subject of the medieval theatre – a unique self-present spectator

> That in his own true circle still doth run,
> And holds his course as certain as the sun.
> He makes it ever day and ever spring
> Where he doth shine, and quickens everything
> Like a new nature; so that true to call
> Him by his title is to say, he's all.

> (*Oberon*,   269–74)

But that is to say that the monstrousness of the comical satires is a specific incompleteness, which is to be healed only by moving out of the public theatre altogether and grounding their structures in the unique performing context of the court masque. There, the relations between humour, character and authority are formalized in the duality of masque and anti-masque; there the offering up of the fiction to the royal spectator who alone can give it meaning is integral to the form; and there the poet, as the dutiful deviser of an entertainment whose ultimate author is taken to be the monarch, is able to borrow the authority which the satirist was struggling to enforce by rhetorical means. In the commercial theatre this drastic centralization is not viable either technically or sociologically. Jonson's development respected that logic. The last of the comical satires was performed in 1601, and when he produced his next comedy, *Volpone*, in 1605–6 he had already written *The Masque of Blackness*, and so embarked on the dual career of masque-writer and dramatist which would be the context of the great comedies of the ensuing decade. The separate stages had different centres, and the persons represented on them had to be constituted in different ways.

The literal truth of that last statement is a factor of some importance. It was in the dramatic parts of Jonson's masques – the dancing was on the floor of the hall – that illusionist stage design was introduced into England. The crucial new technique, brought from Italy by Inigo Jones, was perspective scene painting,[26] which in the context of neo-classicism formed the visual dimension of the ideal of nature: the dramatic unities were complemented by the convergence of the setting on a unitary sense of place. As Stephen Orgel has pointed out, the perspective effect worked perfectly only when viewed from a position in the auditorium exactly opposite the vanishing point; this was of course where the king sat.[27] Everything that happened on the stage contributed to a single harmony for the pleasure of the royal eye, whose form-giving beam it celebrated. As in Velazquez's painting *Las Meninas*, the focus of the image is the royal beholder–and–model.[28]

The Elizabethan playhouse had no equivalent point. The building was circular, with seating occupying perhaps three-quarters of the circle, and a thrust stage projecting roughly as far as the diameter of the ground in the middle.[29] In such a space, it would be impossible for either acting or design to approach the monolinear orientation of a painting: the performance must open out to address a ring of spectators. Because of that multi-directionality, the stage can't have had a single centre. For instance, the point of maximum visibility would be downstage centre – the very middle of the building. But in this position, the actor could see (and therefore speak direct to) only two-thirds of the house at the most. Someone ten feet upstage of him would be in a somewhat less prominent but really more commanding situation; someone at the back wall would in one sense be in the strongest position of all, but too remote from the spectators at ground level to convert that into a strong impression; and so on. Nor is it simply a question of the up–down axis: as in any arena, the radial orientation would make it possible to buy, temporarily, a very intimate contact with one side of the audience by abandoning the other. In short, it was a stage, not with a single fixed centre, but with multiple movable centres; able to operate, not like a painting, but like a spectator sport.[30]

The first act of *Volpone* provides a relatively simple example of the possibilities. The three main legacy-hunters are presented one by one, with Mosca handling each, and Volpone in bed pretending to be ill. The bed is therefore one centre of attention: that is where the money is, in the shape of the supposedly dying testator, and it is also the stage-within-a-stage where Volpone is performing the role of invalid for the benefit of his visitors. But that role is necessarily mostly passive: the centre of the action is with the visitor who is being exhibited, goaded on to ever more extravagant heights of hypocrisy and greed by Mosca in order to amuse Volpone, who rises from his bed in between visits to applaud the performance. Thus if we suppose, as seems likely, that the bed is upstage, and that Mosca brings the visitor down to the front to put him through his paces, then the stage is split into two zones, each of which functions as 'auditorium' to the other's 'stage'.

This decentring of the spectacle through its spatial relations with itself and with the audience is reinforced by another dialogizing factor which is at once vitally important and so obvious that it is often overlooked: laughter. And just as the playhouse stage, while not made inadmissible by any of the rules Jonson regarded as canonical, militated in its characteristic dynamics against the unity of dramatic consciousness which was the canon's underlying principle, so laughter, not proscribed by classicism in the theatre, is nevertheless viewed with great suspicion, even in comedy.

A passage in Jonson's own *Discoveries* puts this very strongly:

> Nor, is the moving of laughter always the end of comedy,
> that is rather a fooling for the people's delight, or their
> fooling. For, as Aristotle says rightly, the moving of

laughter is a fault in comedy, a kind of turpitude, that depraves some part of a man's nature without a disease. As a wry face without pain moves laughter, or a deformed vizard, or a rude clown, dressed in a lady's habit, and using her actions, we dislike, and scorn such representations; which made the ancient philosohers ever think laughter unfitting in a wise man. (*Discoveries*, 3252–64)

As the Oxford editors point out, this is not exactly what Aristotle says. The idea in the *Poetics* is that tragedy represents men as better than they are, comedy as worse, 'in the sense that the ridiculous is a species of ugliness or badness':[31] the fault or turpitude is clearly meant to be in the represented person, not in the comedy as a poem. But the passage in *Discoveries* isn't simply an accidental mistranslation. Comedy, in the sense Aristotle really does imply, is likely to produce images of man that emphasize deformity, ignobility, anomaly. It's not easy to square this with a Horatian ideal of comedy designed according to principles of decorum to instruct and delight. In such a context – which is a specific as well as a general one, for Jonson's text is a free translation of extracts from a contemporary dissertation on Horace's judgement of Terence and Plautus – Aristotle becomes easier to understand if it's assumed that he intends 'ugliness' to convey an aesthetic reservation about a certain type of comedy. The implied distinction between a delightful 'good' comedy and an odious comedy of laughter is drawn out by Sidney in the *Apology for Poetry*: 'Delight hath a joy in it, either permanent or present. Laughter hath only a scornful tickling.'[32]

What strikingly brings Jonson and Sidney together on this is their attribution of the comedy of laughter to the professional theatre. Sidney blames 'naughty play-makers and stage keepers' for the degradation of comedy: 'they stir laughter in sinful things, which are rather execrable than ridiculous; or in miserable, which are rather to be pitied than scorned'.[33] And Jonson follows his source in condemning the travesty of

Socrates in Aristophanes' *Clouds*, adding to it his own implication that buffoonery of this kind is typical of the theatre:
'This was theatrical wit, right stage-jesting, and relishing a
play-house, invented for scorn, and laughter ... This is truly
leaping from the stage to the tumbril again, reducing all wit
to the original dungcart' (*Discoveries*, 3300–13). Here the
classicizing defenders of the drama share terms with the
moralizing pamphleteers against the stage, such as Stephen
Gosson and Philip Stubbes who were after all products of
the same rhetorical humanist education, not the hebraist
philistines of legend. Stubbes's attack on the theatre in *The
Anatomy of Abuses* (1583) is among other things an anthology
of words for the expression of scorn: actors are people who
jest, laugh, fleer, grin, nod, mow, deride, scoff, mock, flout,
jibe.[34].

What this is about formally, as Jonson's contemptuous
reference to the theatre of the streets makes clear, is the
ascendancy of the actor–audience line. Laughter, in the physical sense all these characterizations evoke, is the behaviour
of a crowd: it doesn't figure in the same way in the relation
between a writer and a solitary reader. Moreover, laughter
in the theatre is the medium of a dialogue between the actors
and the audience. Even in a proscenium arch theatre, the
spectators can never be completely removed from the performance so long as the play is funny, because they assert
their presence audibly in a way which penetrates the texture
of the fiction, radically influencing the timing and pointing
of the representation. This in turn arrests the disappearance
of the actor into the 'character', for although he is partly
embroiled in events that happen at Volpone's house or Fawlty
Towers, he is also, evidently, engaged in something which is
happening in the theatre: the business of raising, controlling
and reacting to laughs. It's a significantly different theatrical
situation to that of a drama which intends its audience to be
quiet, because whereas the spectators' consenting silence is
submissive, permitting the fiction to dominate the auditorium
and develop its meanings on its own terms, their laughter is

imperious: while it lasts, the next speaker must wait, and if it is withheld, the effect on the actors is what they concisely refer to as death.

This disproportioning sovereignty of 'the beast, the multitude,' who 'love nothing, that is right, and proper' (*Discoveries*, 3289–91), is clearly what dismays the humanist compiler of *Discoveries*. To play for laughs, to return to the Thespian cart, is to submit all value, all honour and virtue, to the unlimited derision of the crowd. But for the comic playwright, laughter is a necessity, pursued through the action and explicitly offered in prologues and inductions.[35] And in Jonson more than anyone, as we've seen, the laughter is of exactly the scornful kind which the philosophic strictures on it would predict – it's laughter at the anomalous, the ignoble, the diseased, the execrable. Nor is this simply a question of the plays' happening to be funny. In the uncrowned comedy Jonson wrote for the public stage once absolutist characterization had departed to the court, laughter is the key to the constitution of the dramatis personae themselves.

The idea can be found in a marginal fashion in *Every Man In His Humour*. To persuade young Knowell to join him in London, Wellbred writes that he has a present for him: 'our Turkey company never sent the like to the Grand-Signior' (I.ii.73–4). He means two gulls he's cultivating, Matthew and Bobadil; their value as gifts is their potential as objects of laughter. Knowell accepts the invitation and decides to take the melancholy Stephen along with him, explaining in an aside: 'Now, if I can but hold him up to his height, as it is happily begun, it will do well for a suburb-humour: we may hap have a match with the city, and play him for forty pound' (I.iii.106–9). The metaphors from trading and cockfighting suggest a financial project, but in fact Knowell and Wellbred don't exploit their three stooges in any material way. The 'match' remains within a fanciful economics of mirth: the wits are comic entrepreneurs who control the resources of folly, husbanding it and working it up to maximize the output of ludicrous behaviour, and taking their profit in laughter. The gull, striving to enhance his own value in terms of gentility, military prowess, or the like, never notices the surplus value he is producing for his overseer in the form of 'sport'. This system remains suggestive and playful in *Every Man In*, because the play's financial dénouement, Knowell's marriage to a citizen's sister with a three thousand pound portion, is in no way achieved through the use of the gulls. But in *Volpone*, the form comes spectacularly together, as the metaphorical exploitation of scornful comedy is backed by the real thing: Volpone makes fools *and* money out of his clients.

Checking the morning's takings, he remarks,

> Why, this is better than rob churches yet:
> Or fat, by eating, once a month, a man.
>
> (I.v.91–2)

Better, because if from a certain point of view the wealth of churches and the nutritional value of people are both concentrations of resources resulting from greed, Volpone has disdained these secondary accumulations and devised his own organization for tapping the source: his unique swindle is a machine for extracting money from greed itself. As he complacently points out (I.i.30–40), his business doesn't pass through material media such as agriculture, trade, or even usury: his commodity is, directly, human behaviour. The legacy-hunters are his farm, his mine, his fish-pond; he feeds their humours so that the humours will feed him. Thus the exercise of power through knowledge which is 'character' goes far beyond the abstract juridical sadism of the satires. It's a total, appetitive appropriation – a devouring.

Grotesque acts of ingestion and extraction are a recurring feature of the imagery. Mosca speaks of swindlers who

> will swallow
> A melting heir as glibly as your Dutch
> Will pills of butter, and ne'er purge for it.
>
> (I.i.41–3)

Mosca and Corbaccio joke about the latter's present of gold

coins being 'aurum potabile' which will serve Volpone as a
cordial (I.iv.71–6). Volpone, passionate to possess Celia, commits all his possessions to the affair –

> Employ them how thou wilt; nay, coin me, too:
> So thou in this but crown my longings
>
> (II.iv.23–4)

– a hyperbole which matches Mosca's earlier description of
Celia's

> flesh that melteth in the touch to blood!
> Bright as your gold!
>
> (I.v.113–14)

At the centre of this system of exchange is the monstrous
vitality of the allegedly dying man, converting all the other
values in the economy of the play into itself. Even his fear of
detection in the first trial scene takes a physical form: he
confesses afterwards that, suffering from cramp inside his
invalid's disguise, he thought he'd been struck by 'a dead
palsy', and goes on –

> A many of these fears
> Would put me into some villainous disease,
> Should they come thick upon me: I'll prevent 'em.
> Give me a bowl of lusty wine, to fright
> This humour from my heart; [*He drinks*] (hum, hum,
> hum)
> 'Tis almost gone, already: I shall conquer.
> Any device, now, of rare, ingenious knavery,
> Would make me up again! [*Drinks again*] So, so, so, so.
> This heat is life; 'tis blood, by this time.
>
> (V.i.8–16)

The two cures, the wine and the knavery, are intercut in the
speech and its performance, and clearly work in the same
way to restore Volpone's physical substance.

The 'device' he hits upon is to pretend to be dead so as to
enjoy the discomfiture of the hunters. Commentators after the

Restoration were unhappy about this twist of the plot, which is crucial because it leads to the dénouement. The sudden abandonment of the ordinary material motives of the first four acts (money and sex) struck such critics as unnatural.[36] To jeopardize a source of income for the sake of a joke seemed to them an obviously foolish thing to do, which they could not square with the cunning of the Fox. This demand for consistency of character overlooks the physical, erotic immediacy of laughter, the voluptuous satisfaction of working the clients,

> still bearing them in hand,
> Letting the cherry knock against their lips,
> And draw it, by their mouths, and back again
>   (I.i.88–90)

– or, to put it another way, it fails to understand that the constitution of the role of Volpone is *fundamentally* exploitative. It seeks to establish him as a self-enclosed individual who is cunning, self-indulgent, and so on, *first*; and *then* to insert him into an adventure in which he has a bright idea for making money. It retells the story, that is, in terms of an individualist ideology which represents private property as given, and profit as something that happens to it. In Jonson, however, this ideology is, at most, in formation. Individuality is not given in that way, but predicated, as we have seen, by a combative discursive system. What *Volpone* does, by equipping that system with an economic dimension, is to turn it into an image of a competitive society. From the workings of that society, Volpone draws not merely (realistically) his income, but his self-enjoyment, his life-blood, his splendour, his false personae of invalid, mountebank, corpse, commandator – in short, his whole existence as a comic character. It's always the laughing mechanism of exploitation that 'makes up' the man, rather than the other way round.

Elsewhere among the characters, there's a good example of the mechanism at work in the scene where Mosca comes to Corvino to induce him to offer Volpone his wife. Mosca has

explained the medical necessity for the sick man to be supplied
with a young woman, and mentioned that one of the doctors
at the consultation offered his daughter. The dialogue disintegrates into asides:

Corvino   If any man
          But I had had this luck – The thing, in itself,
          I know, is nothing – Wherefore should not I
          As well command my blood and my affections
          As this dull doctor? In the point of honour,
          The cases are all one, of wife, and daughter.
Mosca   I hear him coming.
Corvino   She shall do't: 'tis done.
          Slight, if this doctor, who is not engaged,
          Unless it be for his counsel (which is nothing)
          Offer his daughter, what should I, that am
          So deeply in? I will prevent him: wretch!
          Covetous wretch! Mosca, I have determined.
Mosca   How, sir?
Corvino   We'll make all sure. The party, you wot of,

          Shall be mine own wife, Mosca.
                                      (II.vi.68–81)

The first thing to notice about this writing is its brutal
conciseness as a *psychological* notation. 'If any man but I ...'
means that Corvino's wholly exceptional sensitivity to his
honour as a husband makes it, alas, impossible for him to
seize this opportunity of ingratiating himself with Volpone.
Lesser men might well have fewer scruples in such a case:
it's not that 'the thing itself' is impossible, only that *he* can't
do it. But in the new situation, this strong line on wifely
chastity suddenly appears as a personal weakness in the
struggle for the legacy: the doctor's lack of proper paternal
sensibility is deplorable, no doubt, but it does afford him an
enviable freedom of action, and consequently comes to look
like a kind of strength – the strength of mind, for example,
which is able to conquer one's purely sentimental reluctance

to pimp for members of one's immediate family. Surely Corvino is man enough to control his own feelings of jealousy? Thus the machismo which, just before Mosca's arrival, was constructing a positive bastille of sexual possessiveness reasserts itself to knock away the last prop against its collapse.

What that paraphrase brings out in Corvino's lines is that they work like free indirect discourse: again we see the 'novelistic' way in which Jonson pervades the speech of the dramatis persona with authorial intonations. (The ironically controlled interplay of subtle rationalization and naive egotism is oddly similar to the indirect discourse in Henry James: it's as if the forms which, late in the nineteenth century, start to dismantle the subjective unity of character inadvertently echo those of its prehistory.) To some extent this is done stylistically. 'Covetous wretch!', for example, implies that Corvino is so outraged by the doctor's unscrupulous behaviour that he is more determined than ever to frustrate his scheme by ... a precisely similar scheme of his own: this contradiction is invisible to Corvino, but the actor is invited to make it highly visible to the audience by the rhythmic delay which isolates the phrase and leaves its moralism ludicrously exposed. But Jonson is not leaving everything to the comic skill of the actor. The real condition of the indirectness of the speech is Mosca. It's quite impossible for the audience to identify with Corvino's feelings, because Mosca's presence is a reminder that the doctor, and his daughter, and the whole consultation, have only just been invented. Moreover, Mosca, in a bold break with normal Elizabethan stage convention, can over-hear Corvino's aside, whereas his own is inaudible to Corvino. This means that Corvino's self-consciousness is as it were framed: when we see it, it is already as the object of the cold observation of a spectator on the stage. And what that in turn means, in the detailed progress of the exchange, is that Corvino's verbalized thought process is followed in two contrary directions at once. In the first, Volpone's illness and partial recovery, the doctors' recommendation, and Corvino's precarious status as unconfirmed legatee, all appear as contingencies which Corvino is struggling to meet. That's the reality, if you like, of Corvino's experience, and in responding to it with a decision he is asserting his personality, as is emphasized in the frequent and often metrically stressed repetitions of the word 'I'. But in the other direction, the contingencies all owe their existence to the intention that Corvino should produce just this decision; so that what he thinks is the conclusion of his reflections is really their starting point. So far from asserting himself, he is merging himself step by step into the scenario Mosca has devised for him. In the first direction, Corvino is *going* somewhere, breaking new moral ground with headlong rationalizations; but in the second, Mosca can 'hear him coming' – it isn't uncharted territory after all. Mosca's response to the revelation of Corvino's decision is outrageously frank:

> Sir. The thing,
> (But that I would not seem to counsel you)
> I should have motioned to you, at the first.
>
> (II.vi.81–3)

But the audacity of this admission is more apparent than real. Since the point of the offering is that its merit in Volpone's eyes will be great enough to make Corvino the unchallengeable heir, it's essential that Mosca should carry back to Volpone the news that this was all Corvino's own idea. Even if Mosca had 'seemed to counsel' him more than he has, Corvino would be pretending that he hadn't. Mosca is showing his cards to an opponent who, with what he imagines to be profound cunning, is refusing to look. Thus the alienation injected into the role by the dialogue between the actor playing Corvino and the laughter of the audience is backed and deepened by the derisive and objectifying estrangements of the intrigue.

The delightful thing about this exploitative system from the point of view of the exploiters – and in the same breath the delightful thing about this comic system from the point of view of the audience – is its economy. The dynamism of

the business, so to speak, comes not from its controlling
centre, but from the drive to self-realization of its units, the
persons it *characterizes* by simultaneously drawing them into a
common servitude and separating them from one another.
In producing themselves, with egomaniacal persistence, they
obliviously reproduce the system that makes them up. Only
the lightest touches are needed to keep the mice scrabbling
away at the wheel: their destinies seem almost autonomous
– almost, but not quite:

Volpone   What a rare punishment
          Is avarice to itself!
Mosca   Aye, with our help, sir.
                                              (I.iv.142–3)

His role in this at times makes Mosca himself look like an
autonomous figure: the reality of his selfhood is constantly
being thrown into relief by the hollowness of the selves he
administers. But if he is the most self-possessed of the dramatis
personae – the most conscious, the closest to being a character
– he is also the least. Whenever he is interacting with others,
he is playing a part adapted to their place in the scheme of
things; and when he appears by himself, it's to celebrate his
own limitless variability:

                    I could skip
Out of my skin, now, like a subtle snake,
I am so limber. O! your parasite
Is a most precious thing, dropped from above ...
                                              (III.i.5–8)

Like his gulls, he is not a character, but a function of the
mechanism. The difference is that he is a transcendent
function, the ethereal spirit of the whole – an arrow, a shoot-
ing-star, a swallow, a fly, who can

Present to any humour, all occasion;
And change a visor swifter than a thought!
                                              (28–9)

The edge he has on the others is the completeness of his absence: like them, he has no self-determining identity, but unlike them, he doesn't think he has. He has no material appetites (all he is ever seen to want for himself is money), no home, no authorship even:

Volpone Now very, very pretty: Mosca, this
           Was thy invention?
Mosca   If it please my patron,
           Not else.
Volpone   It doth, good Mosca.
Mosca   Then it was, sir.
                                          (I.ii.63–5)

Nothing he says is true, everything is functional – a *via negativa* of pure exploitation. In the end, when he attempts to stick in one of the roles the mechanism throws out for him – that of Volpone's heir – he is destroyed.

The technical discovery represented by this role is that authorial discourse can penetrate and characterize the persons of the drama without resorting to a directly choric speaker. Mosca is the author's representative in many of his scenes, not discursively – he doesn't enunciate authoritative judgements – but formally; activating types of vice and folly from immediate motives that have less than nothing to do with moralism. The definition of persons in the language of power is still the basic form of characterization, and the attendant splitting of the stage group into objects and commentators is still the underlying principle in the construction of scenes. But now the power is without pretensions to validity; it's simply power; the search for an authenticating monarch is off. The author appears in his play, not as a judge but as a thief, not a scourge but a rip-off artist: the social ordering of subjectivity in the play is fundamentally illicit.

But also, that inversion, as its rhetorical neatness suggests, is possible because the essential structure remains the same. Volpone's house, with its dazzling wealth, its stream of applicants for bounty and its well-established routines for receiving them, is a kind of court, but a travesty court. The king wears a nightcap instead of a crown; the courtiers wish him, not long life, but immediate death; the most favoured suitors are chosen for their exceptional avarice and stupidity; the court masque is a freak show in praise of folly; and so on. The absolutist opposition of the self-identical unity of the monarch and the anarchic plurality of difference is subverted by the older image of an anti-order: not disorder, but misrule.[37] Instead of the normative legality of 'nature', the characters are articulated by a grotesque, disproportioning regime of laughter: the authoritative discourse in which persons are signified is parodic. Hence the fluency and strength of *Volpone*'s use of the multi-directional Elizabethan stage: the theatrical no less than the verbal style is a hybrid, naturally producing game-like scenes that divide the acting area into competing zones; characterizing , not by a monologic descriptive rhetoric which requires to be delivered from a single commanding point, but by the dialogue, generated by laughter, between the actors and the surrounding audience.

Yet if this monstrous, laughing establishment is in part a saturnalian inversion of the real absolutist court for which Jonson wrote the masques, it also rather resembles it:

> As local patronage became more and more concentrated in the hands of the Crown, as tax revenues of the state increased, as the bureaucracy expanded, so the Court became not only the monopolistic centre of political power, but also the market place for the disposal of an ever-increasing volume of cash, pensions, jobs, monopolies, and favours of all kinds.[38]

What made the court, not merely a centre of distribution, but literally a market place, was the Crown's lack of a sufficiently developed tax base to finance this process of centralization; its chronic indebtedness between the 1590s and the eventual collapse of 1642 forced it to exploit court patronage itself as a source of income. The favours – offices, honours, monopolies – were for sale; so was the right to collect certain taxes, and then the right to sell the right. In theory, the state was an extra-economic power, paternalistically controlling the transactions of civil society for the common good, but in practice exemptions from the rules designed to achieve this were for sale as well: under an unconvincing pretence of restraining usury and profit, the court was effectively demanding to be cut in.[39] The rights of private property, although not recognized by political theory, were too well established in real social relations to be accepted as privileges in the gift of the monarch; rather, the property relations permeated the monarch's authority in the covert form of parasitism and corruption – a parodic monetarization of feudal power.[40] This privatization was nowhere more conspicuous than in the immediate environs of the court, for not only was the City of London developing the most powerful bourgeoisie outside the Netherlands, but also, as we saw earlier, the centripetal force of the state itself was pulling together an atomized, individualistic metropolis in which personal identity was alarmingly turned loose from the traditional syntax of church, locality, family and rank, and which sustained such phenomena as 'humours', compulsive gambling, and the commercial theatre.

Jonson, who was of this society as Shakespeare was not, registers it in a negative sense in the remarkable unimportance of kinship in his plays: his significant persons confront the legality that characterizes them alone. But more dynamically, the monetarization of the court is the immediate context for the comic system of his mature comedy. For the travestying inversion is not a carnivalesque crowning of what Bakhtin calls the 'bodily lower stratum', the joyfully devouring and renewing empire of the gut and the genitals, but, much more narrowly, a parodic apotheosis of money. Its cold and abstract utopianism takes the form, not of a saturnalian 'banquet for all the world', but of an infinitely large pile of precious metals.[41] This makes a difference, because the pile, unlike the feast, doesn't mean anything at all outside the socially constituted system of signs which makes it valuable as the property of someone in particular as opposed to anyone else. It isn't elemental or even, centrally, material: it's differentiating, linguistic. This fact is particularly noticeable in *Volpone*, where the hoard that forms the set works in the plot as an ironic double sign – it's what Volpone has got, and also what his clients haven't got.

Thus the coalescence of laughter and money in a single manipulative system is by no means an arbitrary stroke of wit, a merely convenient way of combining the rhetoric of character with an amusing and comprehensible story. It is that, certainly, but it goes beyond it, because the language in which personality is articulated is now not so much poetic or juridical as social: the fantastic inversion bears the trace of a historical revolution. The predication of persons as self-enclosed individual subjects – 'characters' – by the individuating language of private property is something which is happening to the audience too.

Not that this helps Jonson in the theatre of character. For in *Volpone* the individuation is a disease:

These possess wealth, as sick men possess fevers,
Which, trulier, may be said to possess them.
(V.xii.101–2)

The continuing priority of the signifying system over the person signified, of the exploitative mechanism over the exploited consciousness, ensures that Jonson's characters remain divisive, actor-oriented, explosive rather than organic, obstinately refusing to evince the miracle of creation.

3 Languages

It is the misfortune (but also perhaps the voluptuous pleasure) of language not to be able to authenticate itself.[1]

Rather unusually, the plot of *Every Man In His Humour* is set in motion by an act of literary criticism. The intimate letter Wellbred sends to his friend young Knowell is delivered by mistake to the latter's father, who has the same name. Knowell Senior realizes what has happened, but he has heard so much from his son about Wellbred's wit and learning that he can't resist the opportunity to read his letter,

> Be it but for the style's sake, and the phrase,
> To see if both do answer my son's praises.
>
> (I.ii.59–60)

However, as often happens, practical criticism, confronted with an alien text, turns into moral paternalism. Knowell is so disturbed by what he finds in the letter that he decides to follow his son to London and spy on him. This is not because the letter contains any incriminating information, but because of its style, from which Knowell judges the writer to be

> a profane and dissolute wretch;
> Worse, by possession of such great good gifts,
> Being the master of so loose a spirit.
>
> (I.ii.88–90)

Critics in the audience are implicitly invited to compare this drastic judgement with their own, for Knowell reads the letter out:

> Why, Ned, I beseech thee; has thou forsworn all thy friends in the Old Jewry? Or dost thou think us all Jews that inhabit there yet? If thou dost, come over, and but see our frippery: change an old shirt for a whole smock with us. Do not conceive that antipathy between us and Hoxton, as was between Jews and hogs-flesh. Leave thy vigilant father alone, to number over his green apricots, evening and morning o' the north-west wall. An' I had been his son, I had saved him the labour, long since; if, taking in all the young wenches that pass by at the back door, and coddling every kernel of the fruit for 'em, would ha' served. But prithee, come over to me quickly, this morning: I have such a present for thee (our Turkey company never sent the like to the Grand-Signior). One is a rhymer, sir, o' your own batch, your own leaven; but doth think himself Poet-major, o' the town: willing to be shown, and worthy to be seen. The other – I will not venture his description till you come, because I would ha' you make hither with an appetite. If the worst of 'em be not worth your journey, draw your bill of charges, as unconscionable as any Guildhall verdict will give it you, and you shall be allowed your *viaticum*.
>
> *From the* Windmill. (I.ii.63–81)

The neat joke here is that Knowell, having opened the letter in a critical spirit, to assess it as a language object, finds himself described by it in all his 'vigilant' anxiety: the object wittily objectifies him. But that deft reversal is only the leading edge of the more general threat which he perceives in the playfulness of the text as a whole. The language has a miscellaneous allusiveness: there are the fantastic and punning etymologies for place-names, the city bywords about the Levant Company and Guildhall juries, and the flickers of stylistic pastiche – fairground-barker in 'willing to be shown, and worthy to be seen', and commercial-legal in the pseudo-contract of the last sentence. The allusions are densely and specifically London ones – filling out the fact that this is a letter from the city to the country – and this placing is made the more concrete by the saturation of the style in the imagery of trade: the writer briefly adopts the character of an old clothes seller, a pimp, a merchant company, a showman, a cook and a lawyer. The tone Knowell so dislikes is decisively urban, not only in the derisive rusticity of its image of his own life, and not only in the extraordinary concentration of town references, but also in the casual, irresponsible movement from one whimsically chosen topic to the next. The meaning appears to have no firm control over the words: rather, the discourse lets itself be led by the chance associations of language, just as the *flâneur* follows the random energies and juxtapositions of the throng. Knowell's word for it would be 'licentious'; not so much because of the innuendo – though the link between stylistic and sexual looseness is a potent one – as because of a habit of indiscriminate parody which unhinges the proper relationship between thoughts and words. He calls Wellbred a 'gamester', which means a gambler but also, more broadly, one to whom everything is a game.

Thus to the biological opposition (father and son; age and youth) which provides the traditional starting point of his comedy, Jonson adds a *discursive* opposition which is much more historically and culturally specific. It can't exactly be named 'country and city', because although that duality is strongly present, topographically and sociologically, in the action, there's no real attempt to invest Knowell Senior's language in either the moral authority or the mocked naivety which are equally available codes for its rural half. Instead, the role is written in a tone which might be characterized as 'classical wisdom'. In terms of dramatic convention, Knowell is based on the heavy fathers of Roman comedy; moreover, his major soliloquy (in II.v) is, representatively, a tissue of pedagogic precepts from Horace, Juvenal and Quintilian. The part is above all a didactic one, monologically forceful but weak in dialogue, and borrowing the accents of the (Latin-based) nondramatic satire of the play's period. It therefore opposes the street-smart multi-vocality of a Wellbred with the unitary language of paternal authority, coupled with, and universalized by, the cultural authority of classical literature.

At the level of language, in other words, the comic contest of father and son takes the form of what Bakhtin calls the opposition of centripetal and centrifugal tendencies within the word.[2] The centripetal determination of language impels it towards stability, consistency, universality; it entails grammatical and lexical regularity, the proscription of dialectal peculiarities, the hierarchy of genres. It is in tension with the centrifugal force which carries the word away from the language centre towards the object, into the professional, generic, individual and subcultural specifications which limit and fissure its putative universality. Although this is in a sense a transhistorical observation – just something about the way language always works – it's Bakhtin's thesis that the tension is uniquely extreme and dramatic in the linguistic practice of the Renaissance because of the immense ideological labour of unification which was imposed upon the principal European languages and literatures. The interanimation of the languages of conflicting traditions, classes, religions and epochs generated a new order, but also a newly parodic volatility:

At the time when poetry was accomplishing the task of cultural, national and political centralization of the verbal-ideological world in the higher official socio-ideological levels, on the lower levels, on the stages of local fairs and at buffoon spectacles, the heteroglossia of the clown sounded forth, ridiculing all 'languages' and dialects; there developed the literature of the *fabliaux* and *Schwänke*, of street songs, folk sayings, anecdotes, where

there was no language-center at all, where all 'languages'
were masks and where no language could claim to be
an authentic, incontestable face.[3]

The 'heteroglossia of the clown' is a neat summary of what
Wellbred's letter, albeit in somewhat gentrified form, introduces into the play. What the scene enables us to add to
Bakhtin's account is the significance, as a term in his dialectic,
of the city. The size and heterogeneity of Jonson's London –
an outcome, as we saw earlier, of precisely 'national and
political centralization' at the socio-economic level – makes
the centreless interchange of diverse language types a matter
of individual verbal experience. In restricted speech com-
munities, isolated for geographical or institutional reasons
from alien intentions and accents, it may be possible for
language to acquire a convincing air of stability and naturalness; but in the rapidly growing capital, speech types jostle,
relativize and, as both Bakhtin and Jonson emphasize, make
fun of one another. *Every Man In* as a whole is, among other
things, a stylization of such a babel: the idiolects of gallant,
soldier, bourgeois, countryman, street seller, intercut anarch-
ically as the farce gathers momentum. Our letter scene is itself
a nicely economical image of the fortuitous juxtapositions: the
misdirection of the letter reveals that the few hundred yards
between Hoxton and Old Jewry traverse a verbal-ideological
gulf.

This connotation introduces an interesting ambivalence
into the father-and-son comedy. As Glynne Wickham points
out, the Plautine model for the comedy of senior and junior
tended to be inverted by the moralism of the Reformation:
Protestant playwrights, borrowing celebratory plots in which
the wit and vitality of the young win out against the censorious
meanness of their elders, were obliged by the ethical and
religious importance of filial duty to transmute them into
fables of prodigality and forgiveness.[4] Wickham is talking
about mid-sixteenth-century interludes, but the pattern is
continued on the whole in Jacobean city comedies such as

Jonson's own collaboration with Chapman and Marston, *Eastward Ho!* The relationship between the Knowells is not resolved in either direction. The father trails the son, but doesn't succeed in establishing his authority over him, and isn't in any decisive way gulled by him either. Rather, the scheming of the Plautine servant on behalf of the son serves to keep the father out of the action altogether: after its powerful start, the role tails away, and at the end, on discovering that the son has married without his knowledge, he doesn't have a line. There's an exactly similar drift into inconsequentiality in the father-son story in *Poetaster*. The reason, I think, is that Jonson can't find a way of giving either of his sharply conflicting linguistic modes the power to administer and interpret the other; the contest for discursive purchase has to be a draw. The paternal-ethical discourse can characterize the follies of the heteroglot city, trenchantly and eloquently, but from a distance: the very universality of its moral categories disables its intervention in the urban speech world itself. If, on the other hand, that eloquence were to be overwhelmed by the verbal play of the wits and gamesters, then the rhetorical centre of values would be dispersed, and the comedy would become morally incomprehensible. To put it somewhat abstractly: Knowell's predicament poses (as his name suggests) the question of a language for expressing *truth*.

The collection of epigrams which Jonson was apparently writng throughout the years of the major plays, and which he published in the 1616 Folio, calling them 'the ripest of my studies', opens with a couplet 'To the Reader':

> Pray thee, take care, that tak'st my book in hand,
> To read it well: that is, to understand.

> (*Epigrams*, I)

The address is suspicious, unfriendly. Although I have bought the book, it is still Jonson's, and he is warning me about my behaviour in it. There's no promise of a smooth confluence of thought uniting writer and reader: on the contrary, it seems all too possible that now, when the poet has done all he can and must perforce leave his printed words to look after themselves, communication will still fail. The subtle antithesis between taking the book in hand and taking care stresses that possession of the physical volume is not the same thing as possession of its contents. Jonson doesn't trust me to achieve the latter – or, more exactly, he doesn't trust the words. They have no presence, they merely designate thought, their sense is not in them but beyond them in a space where it must be repositioned by a reader: if I fail to do this, the two rhyme words come apart, leaving the writing merely a thing. The text eyes me narrowly because of its need for me. I could spoil everything.

The reason for this precariousness in language is its abstraction. Words don't, by themselves, specify definite things in the world; rather, they demarcate open concepts which close upon particular meanings only in particular contexts. (Jonson's 'Reader', for example, is as it were written blind: it's only when I read it that, without Jonson's knowledge, it wakes up and regards *me*.) The element of indeterminacy thus introduced into the transmission of meaning is a very literal source of danger to the satirist in an absolutist state. Jonson complains tirelessly about the 'politic picklocks' whose ingenious specifications of his satiric generalities could, and occasionally did, lead to his interrogation by the Privy Council.[5] (The complaints do not, of course, mean that the offending applications were not intended.) But the indeterminacy goes beyond the problem of political decipherment. Put at its most extreme, it renders language fictive as a whole. Take for instance another of the collection's two-line conundrums, 'To My Lord Ignorant':

> Thou call'st me poet, as a term of shame:
> But I have my revenge made, in thy name.
>
> (X)

Here Jonson has moved right into the paradoxical zone between concept and application. When the couplet begins,

'My Lord Ignorant' is a fictional character whom the poem dramatically addresses; by the end, it has been revealed that the poem is addressing a real person whom Jonson is *calling* Ignorant by way of retributive insult. This individual is thus caught: the name sticks to him as his personal valuation of the name 'Poet' can't stick to Jonson, because Jonson has used his power as (precisely) a poet to *make* him Lord Ignorant. But the revenge pays for its completeness by its ineffectiveness, since no-one – least of all, perhaps, the ignorant addressee – knows who the poet has in mind. The fictiveness of language affords the poet a profound power to give names; but it also allows particulars to slip away from under the naming, leaving the poetry autotelic, circular.

Throughout the *Epigrams* Jonson struggles, or plays, with this elusiveness of the referent. In 'To My Muse' he curses the muse for having led him to praise 'a worthless lord', but eventually recalls the curse on reflecting that

Whoe'er is raised,
For worth he has not, he is taxed, not praised.

(LXV, 15–16)

The truthfulness of the original encomium is saved as satire having failed as description. 'To True Soldiers' deals with the offence taken at the caricatured Captain in *Poetaster*: Jonson protests how much he reveres true captains and concludes:

He that not trusts me, having vowed thus much,
But's angry for the captain, still: is such.

(CVIII, 9–10)

The implication is that the only captains who still have any reason to object to the offending portrayal are those who resemble it: the epigram uses its inherent circularity to compel assent to itself. In the complimentary epigrams, too, there are comparable attempts to finesse the language into authenticating itself: the poetry assures Cecil that it praises him for the sake, not of his fame, but of its own (XLIII); and Jonson's classical model is told,

Martial, thou gav'st far nobler epigrams
To thy Domitian, than I can my James:
But in my royal subject I pass thee,
Thou flattered'st thine, mine cannot flattered be.

(XXXVI)

The insecurity of all this doesn't come just from the res-
ervations one may have about the particular judgements, nor
even from the consciousness that Jonson is not as naive as he
makes himself look (the jaundiced observers of Tiberius in
Sejanus are well aware of the tactic of flattering by being
unable to flatter).[6] It's that the recurrent metalinguistic conceits speak a fascination with the very possibility they deny
with such wit and precision – that language can perhaps not
be made to denote truly; that all its faces may be masks.

Clearly, doubts of this kind are not simply given by the
existence of language: they aren't experienced by all speakers,
or even by all writers. The question of authentication is posed
as a problem by definite circumstances, definite demands on
language. The formulation by Barthes at the head of this
chapter is a case in point: it emerges from a comparison
between linguistic representation and photography. A photograph, Barthes points out, is evidential; it is literally an
'emanation of the referent'.[7] It's this observation which gives
point to the fact that language is no such thing. Because the
photograph is present in the text as a metaphor, the word's
not authenticating itself ceases to be a simple absence and
acquires the pathos of an unrealized possibility. What is the
equivalent metaphor in Jonson?

The possibility, to restate, is an utterance which would be
self-complete, full of its own meaning and also giving it in
full – which would in short be *true in itself*. What frustrates
the possibility is the unhappy consciousness that the published
word, in a book or a theatre, is incomplete, that it must wait
for its meaning to be taken, and that the taking is very likely
to be partial or even malicious. That's to say: the utterance

can't be true in itself – it can only be true *beyond itself.*

But this is no more than a metaphysical way of saying that language is dialogic. The utopia of the self-complete word is projected out of the problematics of the monologic utterance; that is, of language isolated from its concrete existence as a social practice. That's why the question poses itself where it does: the laconic monumentality of the epigrams, and the didactic pronouncements of the ineffectual fathers, are both in their different ways forms which lift their language out of the play of dialogue and seek to constitute it as authoritative. V.N. Vološinov, working with exactly the same terminology as Bakhtin, points out forcefully that examples of such absolute monologism are not to be found in real, historical language behaviour:

> Any monologic utterance, the written monument included, is an inseverable element of verbal communication. Any utterance – the finished, written utterance not excepted – makes response to something and is calculated to be responded to in turn. It is but one link in a continuous chain of speech performances.[8]

In other words, the monologic utterance is an abstraction. That doesn't mean the concept is empty, but it does mean that it comes into focus as the outcome of a particular point of view.

Vološinov's identification of this point of view is very precise. The postulation of the isolated, finished utterance as the basic unit of language is founded on 'a practical and theoretical focus of attention on the study of defunct, alien languages preserved in written monuments'.[9] A language which no-one any longer speaks exists in the form of a finite number of texts which can't be either altered or added to. At the point of production, obviously, these texts are no more monologic than any other linguistic performance. But within the historically removed culture in which they are studied, they are indeed isolated, finished, and self-complete in the sense that they contain, collectively, all the materials there can be for the construction of their meaning. The indeterminacy which, in a living language, lies between the normative generality of a word and its contextual specification, doesn't affect a dead language, because any given lexical item has already appeared in all the contexts it will ever have. The abstraction of language from social practice has, as it were, been performed by time.

This relationship is of great importance because it appears that dead languages, preserved in sacred or quasi-sacred texts, are to be found at the verbal-ideological heart of very many world-historical civilizations. Certainly in Christian Europe, modern national languages and literatures emerged under the complex hegemony of Hebrew, Greek and Latin. The dead language's abstraction from history renders it immune to dialogization and enables it to function as an authoritative word, the privileged, often magical language of a priesthood, coalescing 'in the depths of the historical consciousness of nations with the idea of authority, the idea of power, the idea of holiness, the idea of truth'.[10]

In Jonson, then, the metaphor by which the dialogism of language is interpreted as a kind of imperfection is Latin. But the case is not a simple one, for Latin in the Renaissance was, as it were, a *newly* ancient language. After the fall of Rome, Latin had survived in the medieval church, which was such an extensive speech community that it sustained it as almost a living tongue, continuing to change semantically, syntactically and so on, though not as rapidly or as radically as the Romance vernaculars. With the humanist rediscovery of republican and Augustan literature, classical Latin was established as the standard from which the language of the church had deviated: this purism, which dismissed contemporary Latin as degraded and corrupt, also inevitably transformed *good* Latin into a dead language. Hence the apparently paradoxical fact that the language of Rome acquired unprecedented prestige at just the moment when new writing of all kinds was departing to the vernacular. Latin was now, in every sense, finished.[11]

What therefore functions in the Renaissance as the supremely valid language is not Latin in general, but specifically the Latin of a limited number of canonical authors. The authority of these in Jonson's cultural environment can hardly be overstated. The study of the grammar, style and content of their writings was virtually the only subject-matter of an ordinary gentleman's education between the ages of seven and seventeen; they provided at once the goal, the curriculum and the criteria for the acquisition of literacy itself.[12] In adulthood it was possible to dissent from their opinions, but from the model of linguistic excellence produced by this prolonged encounter with them there was no appeal. The central discipline in this pedagogy was not poetry – fiction could hardly exercise the kind of authority required – but rhetoric; it was consequently Cicero, as both theorist and practitioner of oratory, as well as moralist, who stood at the summit of the linguistic hierarchy. If any utterance could be true in itself, it was his.

It's scarcely an exaggeration to say that Jonson's tragedy *Catiline* was written to enforce that last proposition. The play is dominated by Cicero's oration in the fourth act, a speech which lasts for about twenty minutes with only occasional one-line interruptions. The duration itself amounts to a qualitative break with the conventions of Jonson's theatre; the whole speech is a bold gesture of faith in the authenticating power of language. It's eloquent – the schemes of Ciceronian oratory are deftly adapted to the rhythms of a long-breathed blank verse which to modern ears inevitably sounds Miltonic – and it's singly decisive in producing the catastrophe of the tragedy. Catiline is expelled from the city, not by executive action, but by the sheer force of rhetoric; and so his conspiracy, a dark and inward threat to the state until this point, is transformed into an open, marginal rebellion, and himself isolated and doomed. The young Caesar, an opportunistic Catilinarian in this play, abandons Catiline in an aside half way through Cicero's performance:

He's lost and gone. His spirits have forsook him.
                                    (*Catiline*.IV.300)

This echoes the prescience of defeat which comes over Shakespeare's Romans. But whereas the departure of their genius
from Brutus or Antony is numinous – at once profound and
whimsical – Catiline's spirits are officially exorcised, mastered
by being eloquently *described*.

Its crucial dramatic function requires the speech to be
'evidential' with a vengeance; Jonson's stylistic means of meeting this requirement is an intense referential directness:

> Here, here, amongst us, our own number, Fathers,
> In this most holy council of the world,
> They are, that seek the spoil of me, of you,
> Of ours, of all; what I can name's too narrow:
> Follow the sun, and find not their ambition.
> These I behold, being Consul; nay, I ask
> Their counsels of the state, as from good patriots:
> Whom it were fit the axe should hew in pieces,
> I not so much as wound, yet, with my voice.
>
> (IV.274–82)

In a sense, the content of this passage amounts to no more
than saying (to translate into a more recent rhetoric) that
there is an enemy within. But the elaboration of the proposition doesn't have the effect of verbiage: rather, the rapid
movement from one 'place' to another (where and who they
are; what they want; what the consul does about them; what
he might do) registers a terseness so extreme that it is itself
a kind of tension. The first two lines, for example, amplify
'here' by moving through the ideas *in this place*; *among these
people*; *members of this group*; *part of this sanctity* – the significance
of the physical and social place where the words are being
uttered is comprehensively detailed in a way which is analytic
rather than grandiloquent. Even the hyperbole of line 278
shares this rigour through being approached in steps: *me*; *you*;
ours; *all*; *more than all*. One logical step ('us') is missing,
and the last one is expressed by a negative periphrasis: the
suggestion is that the words are stretched tight across the

meaning, that this is language with all the referent it can hold. The last two lines are fraught in a more complex way: the double antithesis ('hew in pieces' against 'not ... wound', and 'axe' against 'voice') gives a very strong and symmetrical declaration of Cicero's lenity, which is broken open again, just before its syntactic completion, by the intrusive and suggestive 'yet'.

This is consciously exemplary style, copious enough to expatiate on the topic in full, yet, equally, full of the topic, without redundancy. The formal goal is perspicuity: that is, the words are to have no autonomy, no opacity, no internal contradictions – no *history*, we could say – but to function purely as instruments of the power of the mind. This hierarchical duality, a sort of linguistic Cartesianism, is variously theorized in Jonson's pedagogic writings. For example:

Speech is the only⋅benefit man hath to express his excellency of mind above other creatures. It is the instrument of society. Therefore Mercury, who is the president of language, is called *deorum hominumque interpres*. In all speech, words and sense are as the body, and the soul. The sense is as the life and soul of language, without which all words are dead. (*Discoveries*, 2328–36)

The acoustic and graphic forms of language are dead matter; it's the sense, invisibly within or beyond them, that gives them life and reason. It's easy to see how well this monologic conception of speech fits a linguistics centred on a dead language (Jonson is here paraphrasing, not a classical author, but a sixteenth-century humanist). Again:

The conceits of the mind are the pictures of things, and the tongue is the interpreter of those pictures. The order of God's creatures in themselves, is not only admirable, and glorious, but eloquent: then he who could apprehend the consequence of things in their truth, and utter his apprehensions as truly, were the best writer or speaker. (*Discoveries*, 2635–42)

God – the order of things – the picture of it in the mind – the verbal interpretation of the picture: the function of each link in the descending chain is simply to be faithful to the signification of the one above.

The speech in *Catiline* is unusually well adapted to this model because of its status as a translation. It's a fairly faithful English version of the historical Cicero's first oration *In Catilinam*,[13] a well known grammar school text, as Jonson points out. The combination of copiousness and conciseness that marks the style is technically possible because of the derivative Latinism of the syntax. 'Here ... they are, that ...' is 'Hic sunt ... qui ...'; 'These I behold, being Consul' is 'Hos ego video consul', and so on. Elsewhere in the speech, vocabulary behaves in the same way: 'oppress', 'convent', 'persuade', 'note' and many other words are used in contexts which dictate their root sense in Latin. The translation works, not only to convey the content of what Cicero said to an English-speaking audience, but also to Latinize the English spoken in the scene. The lines of the stage Cicero therefore carry the signs of their extra-dramatic origin like an official badge. The words dominate the fictive construction in which they are spoken because the speaker is also, conspicuously, the author's author.

At one level, what this emphasizes is the authenticity of documentary. The audience hears, as nearly as possible, what the Senate of Rome actually heard in the temple of Jupiter Stator on 8 November, 63 B.C. This is part of the point of the oration's length: immense by the standards of the theatre, it's quite modest for a *real* speech. But the relative banality of that kind of truth is indicated by the reflection that it would have been yet more complete if it had been possible (in a university performance, for example) simply to stage the original. Clearly this would not have exerted the authority which the device requires; for, as I've said, it can't be the case that there's anything uniquely referential about the Latin text 'itself'. Its authority is inseparable from its dehistoricizing

mode of insertion into the vernacular: that is what makes it
classical, and it is thus – as a metaphor of linguistic completeness *for English* – that it figures in the play.

Above all, the meeting-point of the classical language and
the vernacular is the place where meaning is withdrawn from
the vagaries of context and invested in the fixity which is
essential if the speaker is to be able to 'utter his apprehensions … truly'.

> The philologist–linguist, when comparing different con-
> texts in which a word appears, focuses his attention on
> the identity factor in its usage, since to him what is
> important is to be able to remove the word from the
> contexts compared and to give it definition outside con-
> text … This process of isolating a word and fixing its
> meaning outside any context takes on added force when
> comparing different languages, i.e., when trying to
> match a word with an equivalent word in another lan-
> guage. In the process of linguistic treatment, meaning
> is constructed, as it were, on the border of at least two
> languages. These endeavors on the linguist's part are
> further complicated by the fact that he creates the fiction
> of a single and actual object corresponding to the given
> word. This object, being single and self-identical, is just
> what ensures the unity of meaning.[14]

In other words, the effect of the philological encounter is to
reify the semanticity of the languages involved. Between the
two, a *thing* appears – the 'single and self-identical' *realia*, the
objective content of the translator's having got it right—which
is then immediately represented as the extra-linguistic origin
of the word's unity of meaning: the thought, of which the
word is the true utterance. (The soul of which it is the body,
the monarch of which it is the ambassador.)

However, this object, to which the word stably and fully
corresponds, is, as Vološinov roundly says, a fiction. The

sovereignty of the rhetoric is secured by the ideological work of subordinating its verbal environment to it: it's not really that meaning is fixed independently of context, but that the context is itself, so to speak, fixed. The image of a language that escapes the curse of fictiveness is projected out of a fictive structure: a plot.

First of all, the political crisis at which the oration is delivered is such that Cicero's knowing about the matters he describes is itself decisive. There is a conspiracy; concealment is essential to it; Cicero, the conspirators' prime target, is the person from whom it must above all be concealed. His describing it therefore does have evidential force, for special reasons: firstly because it *proves* to the conspirators that they have been betrayed, and later because revealing the fact forces them into counter-measures which demonstrate to everyone the truth of what has been said. A unique applicability has thus been procured for the speech by the occasioning situation.

It's a deep-laid *coup de théâtre*, but it isn't without its contradictions. Although it's part of the rhetorical triumph that the speech represents its indefeasibility as the general condition of the discourse of the state, the course of the drama not only depicts the particular means of Cicero's advantage, but rather insists on their sordidness. The conspiracy was betrayed to Fulvia, a pretentious and trivial-minded whore, by her brutal lover Curius: having extracted his secret by blatant sexual teasing, she passed it on to Cicero because she was jealous of another *demi-mondaine* who was in on it. In the scene where he learns of it, Cicero praises Fulvia's patriotism in extravagant and appropriate terms:

> Here is a lady, that hath got the start
> In piety of us all; and for whose virtue
> I could almost turn lover again: but that
> Terentia would be jealous.

> (III.341–4)

But once he has engaged the pair as informers and they

have left, Cicero apostrophizes Rome, lamenting the city's humiliation in that the symptoms of its sickness

> should not rise out
> From any worthy member, but a base
> And common strumpet, worthless to be named
> A hair or part of thee.

(III.449–52)

The grossness of the flattery of Fulvia measured, then, not naivety but contempt: the great orator was producing 'bad' rhetoric with bitter, private irony. The lapidary authority of the oration is shown to be constructed out of some much more partial and conflictual intonations, and this impugns, marginally, its claims to completeness.

Oratory confronts a more formidable otherness in the figure who sits through the oration, silent and maximally conspicuous: Catiline himself. At the end, finding himself isolated, he accepts his informal expulsion:

Catiline Well, I will leave you, Fathers; I will go.
      But– my fine dainty speaker – [*He turns suddenly on Cicero*]
Cicero   What now, Fury?
      Wilt thou assault me here?
(Chorus   Help, aid the Consul.)
Catiline See, Fathers, laugh you not? Who threatened him?

(IV.490–3)

Catiline's retort to twenty minutes of magnificent denunciation is a single instant of physical dangerousness, which in its lightness, its casual hint of latent reserves of violence, mocks not only Cicero, but the entire culture of eloquence which, as we have seen, he supremely represents. The moment of silence concentrates in a sort of theatrical epigram Catiline's role in the tragedy, which, despite its volubility, is radically anti-discursive. The excesses of the part, from the casual murder of a slave to provide real blood for the conspiratorial oath, to the cynical anti-oratorical oratory of the speech before the last battle, construct it as the antithesis of Cicero's – doing against speaking, personal appetite against universal judgement, the body against thought. That his death is reported in a monumental narrative speech not only fits the classical decorum Jonson has adopted, but also deepens Catiline's essential silence: his prodigious culmination figures as the wordless object of a messenger's eloquence; he dies beyond words. Language is authenticated, but – this is what makes the play a tragedy – a different kind of authenticity, biological, barbaric, continues to elude its closure.

This is by no means an abstract opposition between the verbal and the existential in general. It's made very explicit that Catiline's dependence on the sword has to do with his social alienation as an impoverished patrician, while Cicero's complementary reliance on the word is that of a 'burgess' son' (IV.480) raised to greatness by talent and 'virtue'. Implicit in Catiline's exploitation of his own presence is an aristocratic code of personal courage and physical integrity; implicit in Cicero's rhetoric is a juridical code committed to the equality of citizens before the senate and people of Rome. Politically, therefore, the confrontation of the two different types of authenticity is a struggle between two kinds of social order. Cicero's power is that of a 'new man', a function of the ideological centralization of the state: the speech in which he accepts the consulship emphasizes, with a mixture of humility and arrogance, his lack of noble ancestors and his consequent dependence on his own virtue and patriotism, to make the point that, having no independent stature, he is as it were obliged to be public-spirited (III.1–45). Catiline's rebellion in these terms, is precisely the assertion of a personal greatness independent of the value-conferring discourse of the state. The terms on which he is a son of Rome are not universal and ethical, but individual and organic:

Was I a man, bred great as Rome herself?
One, formed for all her honours, all her glories?
Equal to all her titles? ...

And was I,
Of all her brood, marked out for the repulse
By her no voice, when I stood candidate ... ?
If she can lose her nature, I can lose
My piety; and in her stony entrails
Dig me a seat where I will live again,
The labour of her womb ...

(I.83–95)

The image of Rome as the great mother is present in Cicero's
rhetoric too, but it is purely formal and respectful: it refers
to the social institution of motherhood and the rights attached
to it. This is quite different: the relationship is passionately
physical; an electoral defeat is a primal rejection and a *coup
d'état* an Oedipal rape. Thus whereas for Cicero social power
is an impersonal instrument, easily passing from one relatively
unimportant individual to another, for Catiline it is an inalien-
able property, part of one's identity, even of one's body.

Whatever its validity as ancient history, this opposition is
one that seizes on the Catilinarian conspiracy for Jonson's
own age. The appropriation has been argued in great detail
by Basil De Luna:[15] Cicero is Cecil, Catiline Catesby, Sulla
Essex, the conspiracy the Powder Plot, and so on. In its
particulars, this key requires implausible ingenuity; but it's
certainly true that the making of correspondences was a
central procedure of Elizabethan historiography, and that
Jonson's play makes this one at least available. And certainly,
too, the defeat of the plots of 1601, 1603 and 1605 was,
taken together, a victory for the bureaucratic power controlled
by the Cecils over the politics of personal attachment and
violent prowess. However, the historical content of the structure of *Catiline* can't really be reduced to these personal
matchings. For what was happenng epochally, between 1570
and 1620, was a redefinition of aristocratic power which at
once demilitarized it and subordinated it to the presiding
authority of the sovereign. Aristocratic resources were trans-
ferred from the maintenance of paramilitary retainers to the

pursuit of influence at Court; the lawsuit replaced the feud as the medium of conflict between landed families; an educational revolution eradicated ruling-class illiteracy and replaced the castle and the sword with the office and the pen as the instruments of social hegemony. Above all, the systematic enforcement of the Elizabethan religious settlement imposed something like a state monopoly in social ideology, marginalizing the sub-national loyalties on which the baronial dynasties had founded their power, and forging an intimate link between political and confessional conformity, sedition and atheism.[16]

Thus when, in Jonson's play, Cicero routs Catiline by talking, he is acting as a 'new man' in more than a narrowly biographical sense. He is speaking, to put it schematically, for the absolutist present against the feudal past. But that is not to say that Catiline is a representative of the old order in any historicist way. Rather, with his familiar ghost and his bad heroism, he is the old order represented within a linguistic world (the world of the play) where the centralizing ideology of the state is *already the truth*. He is a conspirator, an incendiary, a voluptuary; his feudalism is vestigial, rendered demented and death-obsessed by the universal scope of the Ciceronian discourse: against Rome, there is no longer anything to be but evil. Or, more rigorously: it is the function, within the text, of his evil to render the discourse universal; his madness and deadliness are its rationality and life.

Thus the enabling term in the authentication of speech turns out to be the centralization of the state: the authority of language is underwritten by the language of authority. The idea of a self-complete and effectual language is realized with great artistic strength, but its price is a far-reaching and political polarization of the centripetal and centrifugal impulses within the word. Heteroglossia is criminalized.

Just as 'crime' is a diversity of behaviours collected under a single sign by the singleness of the legality which defines itself by making them its other, so the polarization of the word constructs from the diversity of speech-types the idea of a unified antithetic language – a paradoxical eccentric centre. The age, and Jonson in particular, had a name for this linguistic abstraction: canting.

An odd mixture of dialect, Romany and urban slang, canting was outlaw speech in two ways. It was supposed to be spoken by vagabonds, pimps, con-men and thieves; and also, because of the nefarious purposes of these groups, it deliberately obscured its meanings. In the cony-catching pamphlets which are the documentary source for it, this underworld language has an improbable degree of regularity and cohesion: it seems clear that the accounts of it are not a simple sociological record, but have the form of a comic-monitory mirror-image of legitimate society, one strand in the popular literature of 'the world turned upside down'.[17]

The image of canting runs right through Jonson's dramatic language. It's most conspicuous and schematic in the court entertainments, where the opposition between the authoritative language and the abstract counter-word is absorbed into the logic of masque and antimasque. This is a complementary opposition rather than a conflictual one. The masque proper, a unified spectacle composed of scenic and costume design, music, poetry and, most centrally, dancing, is definingly a vision of perfection – of unalloyed harmony, beauty and truth – conceived of as emanating from the person of the monarch. The essential function of the antimasque is therefore to represent the imperfection which the masque perfects: if it is discordant, grotesque, delusive, this is in order not to pose even the most bracketed challenge to the eventual unity but merely to provide the dramatic syntax, so to speak, in which perfection can be staged as an event. The language of antimasque is consequently deformed and incomplete *as such*: its own deviance is its most important signified. Over the years, Jonson fills this space with a bizarre variety of marginal speech-types. The canting vocabulary of the vagabond literature appears directly in *The Gypsies Metamorphosed*,

but comparable aims are served elsewhere by somewhat parodied Welsh and Irish dialects, by the jargons of witchcraft
and alchemy, by a Rabelaisian rhetoric of the bottle and the
belly,[18] and, most remarkably and representatively, the
speech of Fant'sy in *The Vision of Delight*, which, as the Yale
editor observes, free-associates moral emblems to produce a
verbal equivalent of a Bosch painting:

> If a dream should come in now to make you afeard,
> With a windmill on his head and bells at his beard,
> Would you straight wear your spectacles here at your
>   toes,
> And your boots o' your brows, and your spurs o' your
>   nose?
> Your whale he will swallow a hogshead for a pill;
> But the maker o' the mousetrap is he that hath skill ...
>   (*Vision of Delight*, 71–6)

A train of thought of a kind can apparently be recovered from
the speech, but in performance it must effectively be dispersed
in the jostle of phantasmagoric visual images. It's all but
autonomous writing, words appearing to cut loose from the
subordination to 'sense' enjoined on them by the dualistic
ideal of perspicuity. Designedly, the contrast with the lucid
propriety and economy of the lyrics which close the masque
is as extreme as possible:

Aurora I was not wearier where I lay
>   By frozen Tithon's side tonight,
>   Than I am willing now to stay
>   And be a part of your delight.
>   But I am urged by the day,
>   Against my will, to bid you come away.
>   (222–7)

Equally typically, it's a metrical contrast: antimasque is characterized by couplets of grotesquely long or short lines, by
lumpy street-ballad anapaestics of the kind Fant'sy speaks,
by doggerel and by colloquial prose; masque by speeches in

heroic couplets and fluidly strophic lyrics. The effect of this opposition precisely matches that which controls the imagery: whereas the words of the masque seem to arise spontaneously from what they signify (that is, ultimately, from the king), the words of the antimasque get stuck in their lexical and acoustic particularity, whose relationship with signification remains tenuous and problematic. In short, 'sense' becomes entangled in the *materiality of the signifier*.

Both the tragedy and the masques provide a very clear and rigid formula for the polarity of centripetal and centrifugal verbal tendencies; the one by making it into a political, violent and decisive conflict, the other by means of a stylized centripetal structure which excludes conflict altogether. In the comedies, the materiality of the signifier is an altogether more volatile and contradictory affair.

In the comical satire *Cynthia's Revels*, for example, the recherché composite style of the courtiers' speech reflects, authorially, the futility of their existence: nothing but the turbid redundancy of their language protects them from their own emptiness. This approaches the point of self-parody when, waiting with parched lips for their servants to bring them supplies of water from the fountain of self-love, they pass the time with word games. In the first, 'Substantives and Adjectives', one player thinks of a noun but doesn't reveal it, and then each of the others thinks of an adjective and announces it. The noun is then revealed, and each player has to justify the aptness to it of the modifier he chose in ignorance. The second game is concisely explained in the text:

> I imagine, A thing done; Hedon thinks, Who did it; Moria, With what it was done; Anaides, Where it was done; Argurion, When it was done; Amorphus, For what cause it was done; you Philautia, What followed upon the doing of it; and this gentleman, Who would have done it better. (IV.iii.142–6)

The point of the game is that this narrative order is reversed in the playing, so that 'who could have done it better' is announced first, and what 'it' was only after all the other players have committed themselves to the supplementary details.

The games are mechanisms for inverting the proper hierarchy of thought and language: instead of words serving as the emissaries or embodiments of the speaker's apprehensions, the apprehensions are generated accidentally by words chosen at random. If, as Jonson says in *Discoveries*, sense is the soul of language and words the body, then the courtiers are fooling about with linguistic zombies. It's that hint of perversion which motivates the violent authorial denunciations of amusements which, like this one, often seem no more than harmlessly silly. Language is supposed to do honour to the mind it represents, as a royal court is supposed to do honour to the sovereign it expresses: these courtiers profane both dignities, and each sacrilege is a metaphor for the other. However, the denunciations, tensely voiced by the play's authorial spokesman Crites, also speak an anxiety which can't altogether be acknowleged. The elements of the games are, after all, rhetorical: the first requires the players to improvise a case within certain assumptions about the propriety of epithets, and the second is a version, only mildly travestied, of the rhetorical discipline of *inventio*, the finding out of 'matter' for an oration by the use of a set scheme of topics.[19] Rhetoric, the classical system of theory and practice which sustains the authority of the Ciceronian ideal, also produces the senseless utterances which are its negation. The dignity of speech is subverted, not by the incursion of some wholly alien patois, but from within.

This contradiction keeps surfacing in the comedies. In *Bartholomew Fair* a vein of half-gratuitous verbal combat and vituperation culminates in another game, 'Vapours', which consists simply of each player contradicting whatever has just been said: the scene is at once a head-banging negation of meaning and a parody of academic disputation.[20] *Volpone*, on a slightly different plane, features a series of cant orations – the speeches of Nano, Castrone and Androgyno in praise of

folly and deformity, Volpone's own masquerade as Scoto
the mountebank, and Voltore's judicial oration, a superb
exhibition of rhetorical skill successfully aimed at producing
a comprehensive miscarriage of justice. What immediately
underlies these more or less cynical formalisms is a contradiction in the rhetorical heritage itself. It's that the self-
complete language in which the state enunciates its truth is
only one face of Ciceronianism. Rhetoric is also a compendium
of verbal and persuasive devices which can be (and were)
tabulated and taught as autonomous techniques, without reference to truth values of any kind.[21] So far from regularizing
and underwriting the referentiality of language, rhetoric in
this sense tends, both in theory and in practice, to redirect
verbal energy away from reference; to thicken words, as it
were, rendering them free-standing and opaque.

The comedies produce this contradiction as a persistent
speech-type which can best be described as linguistic *junk* –
that is, a cultural object ambivalently compounded of alienation, bad taste, cheapness, freedom, fun, superabundance,
uselessness, waste. The more judgemental and authoritarian
the comic structure, the nastier and sillier the junk. In
Poetaster, for example, the last of the 'War of the Theatres'
plays, Jonson–Horace administers a poetic pill to Marston–Crispinus which causes him to vomit the indigestible
words that have been clogging his system; 'turgidous', 'ven-
tositous', 'oblatrant', 'furibund', etc. come up amid much
groaning and are caught in a basin (V.iii.365–479): the
insistence on the materiality of the signifier could hardly be
more negative. At the other end of Jonson's career, in *The
Staple of News*, a father who pretends to have died so as to
test the prudence of his heir observes the progress of his
experiment in the persona of a 'Canter', an eccentric and
beggarly disguise which functions as a satiric mask. At the
climax of this plot (IV.iv), the Canter undertakes to show
that all the prodigal's mercenary associates are themselves
canters. Herald, doctor, soldier, poet and courtier in turn
have their specialist jargons parodied, placed, and dismissed

as canting. The heir is enchanted by this vision of universal nonsense, and proposes to found, with the assistance of the Lady Pecunia, a Canters' College in which everyone will profess his own self-enclosed and unintelligible discourse. Although this idea forces us to credit Jonson with a certain historical clairvoyance, it remains inertly theoretical within the play: such dramatic vitality as it does promise is immediately closed off by the Canter's unmasking and asserting his legal authority as a father. It's a decisively reactionary resolution of the stalemate of paternal monologism and filial heteroglossia which was set out a generation earlier in *Every Man In*, and one which is made possible only by a very masque-like movement of abstraction: in Pecunia, the environment of the seductive, dealing city is summarized in the allegorical person of Money.

It's in the intervening masterpieces that junk language really functions as a dramatic medium: *Epicoene*, with Truewit's Wildean commitment to superficiality and the macaronic babble of Otter and Daw; *Bartholomew Fair*, with the competing cants of fairground, puritan and justice, and the climactic doggerel of the puppet play; and, most concentrated of all, *The Alchemist*, whose fourth act is the linguistic equivalent of a riot. Face has the fantastical innuendo which is the role's staple, as well as the increasingly incoherent alchemical terminology he shares with Subtle, who also, in one of the scenes, is heard blinding Kastril with the science of quarrelling. Dol pretends to have gone mad, and enters uttering an unstoppable stream of incomprehensible extracts from a work of millenarian theology. Surly, who appeared earlier to be the voice of common sense in the play, spends half the act pretending not to be able to speak anything but Spanish; and when he reveals his true identity, he is swept from the stage by the sub-Biblical rhetoric of Ananias and the indiscriminate aggression of Kastril, whose vocabulary of abuse includes several otherwise unrecorded words which probably don't mean anything at all. It's an exhibition of rhetorical productivity unfettered and unsupported by any category of representational truth: the multiplying cants and idiolects, even when they aren't complete nonsense, refer to objects which don't exist. In the middle of the act the offstage chemical experiment (which doesn't exist) blows up with a loud bang; the image is an appropriate one; at this extreme point of comic travesty, the rigid centripetal order of Jonson's language ensures that its centrifugal energy is released in the form of an explosion.

Thus the comic corollary of Jonson's linguistic classicism is a hypersensitive consciousness of the anarchic and unverifiable plurality of the vernacular. Living speech, speech as polymorphous social interaction, appears by the dry light of the absolutist Latin ideal to be a monster, endlessly doubling, compartmentalizing, contradicting and parodying itself, travelling ever further outwards, in its illicit dynamism, from some pristine centre of truth and sense. A casual comment of Tennyson's – 'I can't read Ben Jonson, especially his comedies. To me he appears to move in a wide sea of glue.'[22] – registers with accurate distaste the insistent materiality of the language the opposition produces. On the seamy side of Mercury, *deorum hominumque interpres* but also the patron of lying and thieving, words are deception, junk, noise.

The panic thus induced is grotesquely staged in the figure of Morose, the 'gentleman that loves no noise' in *Epicoene*. He is, programmatically, the monster's peculiar victim:

Epicoene You are not well, sir! You look very ill! Something
            has distempered you.
Morose   Oh, horrible, monstrous impertinencies! Would
            not one of these have served?

                                        (*Epicoene*, IV.iv.28–31)

Morose on the stage is an alienation device. His whole life is a monomanic campaign to reduce acoustic signs of all kinds to their absolute semantic core, to establish a *cordon sanitaire* of silence between himself and the linguistic environment of the city. Fishwives, sweeps, metal-workers, street musicians, bear-wards and passing bells all appear, abstracted from their social and communicative functions, as malevolent threats to his peace of mind; London, seen from this peculiar angle, is essentially a cacophony. And since a theatrical performance is itself something which entails making a good deal of noise, Morose is an impediment to the whole process of the play in which he finds himself. His obsession is an arbitrary slash through the dramatic text, separating its meanings from its materiality. At the climax of the plot he cries in anguish, 'Oh, my heart! Wilt thou break? ... Marry a whore! And so much noise!' (V.iv.125–7): the line is funny because of its unexpected move across the slash.

Tacked on to that arbitrariness, though, is a surprisingly naturalistic explanation for Morose's phobia:

> My father, in my education, was wont to advise me, that I should always collect, and contain my mind, not suffering it to flow loosely: that I should look to what things were necessary to the carriage of my life, and what not: embracing the one, and eschewing the other. In short, that I should endear myself to rest, and avoid turmoil: which now is grown to be another nature to me. (V.iii.42–7)

The terms of this opposition – control, propriety, rest, against looseness, impertinence, turmoil – are precisely those of the opposition between Hoxton and Old Jewry in *Every Man In*; it's not surprising that Morose links them, once again, to the motif of fatherly wisdom. The same cluster of values appears, untouched by the ironies of the comic theatre, in Jonson's *Epitaph on Master Vincent Corbet*. The poem honours Corbet as a 'friend and father', and praises

> the just canon of his life,
> A life that knew nor noise, nor strife:
> But was by sweetening so his will,
> All order, and disposure, still.
> His mind as pure, and neatly kept,
> As were his nurseries; and swept

So of uncleanness, or offence,
That never came ill odour thence.

(Underwoods, XII, 11–18)

It's noticeable that in this case, as in old Knowell's, the calm quiet centre, from which the looseness and lightness can be reproved, is associated with the idea of the garden, which connotes, whether through the Garden of Eden or the Sabine Farm of Horace, idyllic detachment from the enmeshing social forces which fragment and falsify the monologic word. The unfortunate Morose is without any such objective grounding for his habits of 'order, and disposure', and tries to impose them on a 'noisy', heteroglot environment by a unilateral gesture which consequently renders them shrill and rigid. The outcome is a rough, reductive parody of the monologistic father-figure: a mean old man who can't stand anyone talking except himself. As such, Morose is caught in a sharp, farcical irony: the passionate singleness of his attempts to get everyone else to shut up creates the conflict which motivates the crescendo of babble which is the plot. Language for him is like a punchbag: the harder he pushes it from him, the harder it comes back and hits him in the face.

Tormented by his talkative bride, for example, he curses the barber who helped to arrange the marriage: 'May he get the itch, and his shop so lousy as no man dare come at him ...' (III.v.62–3). Truewit enthusiastically joins in, and it becomes a sort of antiphonal execration:

Morose Let him be glad to eat his sponge for bread.
Truewit And drink *lotium* to it, and much good do him.
Morose Or for want of bread –
Truewit Eat ear-wax, sir. I'll help you. Or draw his own
　　　　teeth, and add them to the lute-string.
Morose No, beat the old ones to powder, and make bread
　　　　of them.
Truewit (Yes, make meal o' the millstones.) (76–82)

Morose set the curse going, but it seems to acquire a momentum of its own, escaping from his intention. For Truewit

it becomes a game like the ones in *Cynthia's Revels*: what
punishments would be appropriate for a barber? For Morose
it's like a nightmare: his rage against talk is generating more
talk:

Truewit ... that he be never able to new-paint his pole –
Morose Good sir, no more. I forgot myself.
Truewit Or want credit to take up with a comb-maker –
Morose No more, sir.
Truewit Or having broke his glass in a former despair, fall
            now into a much greater of ever getting
            another –
Morose I beseech you sir, no more.
Truewit Or that he never be trusted with the trimming of
            any but chimney-sweepers – (91–100)

Flailing in the 'wide sea of glue', Morose can neither get
ashore nor drown. The cacophony is inescapable, because it
really is, too, the element of social existence: to transcend it,
one would have to be dead, like Latin.

    Yet Morose's discomfiture in the play never amounts to a
positive affirmation of linguistic pluralism: the speech community from which he is expelled at the end of the comedy
is anything but natural or reconciled. The decisive moment
is the removal of Epicoene's wig to reveal that she is a boy.
This action dissolves Morose's misalliance and completes his
humiliation, but it simultaneously provides an equally cruel
dénouement for the other two plots. The college of women is
exploded because its secrets have been penetrated by a male;
and the gulls, Sir Amorous La-Fool and Sir John Daw, are
exploded because they have just admitted, with assumed
reluctance, that they both slept with Epicoene before she was
married. None of these people whose situations are transformed by the unmasking says anything at all: it literally
brings their roles to an end. The point of this *coup de théâtre* is
that it releases truth from language altogether: the characters
concerned are struck dumb, and not merely by a verbal

representation which is more convincing than their own, but by a demonstration which is incontestable because it is wordless. In this, the scene is a paradigm for the endings of all the great heteroglot comedies: Volpone 'uncases' in open court and the labyrinthine play of rival versions of reality collapses like a house of cards; the proliferating imaginary worlds of *The Alchemist* are blown away by the non-negotiable fact of Lovewit's return; at the end of *Bartholomew Fair* Justice Overdo's wordy and inaccurate exposures culminate in the discovery that one of the whores is his own wife, and in an anti-discursive stage-direction even more emphatic than the one in *Catiline*, 'her husband is silenced'.

This 'silencing' is – rather than marriage – the characteristic Jonsonian comedy ending.[23] And whereas the Shakespearean marital resolution makes a harmony of language and nature through the healing fusion of institutional and creatural categories, Jonson's coercive unmaskings fix a sceptical space between words and things. The things, finally uncovered in their flat and speechless identity, show up the opacity, the incurable fictiveness, of the words. Thus, perversely, Morose is vindicated. The torrent of articulate sound which has been sweeping over him since the play began is indeed impertinency, clatter, unnecessary tumult. But the endorsement does him no good. He is still defeated, still a freak; it's still apparent that his project of imposing a monologic stasis on his environment is impractical and deranged. Canting accompanies language inescapably – no signal without noise, no image without distortion. It can't be thrown away, because it has been thrown away already; that is the condition of its atrocious freedom.

4 Theatre

The rhetorical functionalism which divides language into message and noise, sense and babble, soul and matter, is inevitably embarrassed by theatre itself. For if the materiality of the verbal signifier is in the last resort inescapable, that of the theatrical signifier is positively ostentatious; not only in the form of paint, costumes, timber, canvas and the rest of the lumbering devices from which we saw Jonson distancing his poetry in the *Every Man In* prologue, but still more in the physically and historically actual person of the actor. However completely the dramatic text can be integrated with the authority of a monologic humanism, theatrical classicism must continue to be disturbed by the inauthentic being who speaks its words and so, in giving over his body to the significations of others, makes himself something both more and less than human.

This is by no means a universal problem of the theatre. Historically, most theatrical forms have accorded some definite status to the gesture – putting on a costume, for example – whereby the actor assumes a role. In medieval religious theatre, he is a kind of celebrant, his entering the role a special type of robing. In many hieratic theatres, putting on one's costume is itself a ritual, governed by the same magical systems which structure the performance itself.[1] In modern agitational theatre, costume conventionally affords only a

minimal and easily penetrable disguise: the actor is under-
stood not to be giving his body to the role, but only lending
it for the time it takes to 'make the point' within the discourse
of the collective of which he remains a member. In all these
cases, the cultural context of performance is such (whether
it's the sacred categories of a religion, the hierarchical ones
of a feudal society, or the dialectical ones of a political struggle) that real events and persons happen on several levels,
and performers can move from one level to another without
giving rise to anxiety. There's a problem only when the
socially given codes which are the theatre's point of departure
posit a monolinear conception of reality, leaving the performance with nothing to do but to represent that reality, and
nothing to *be* but unreal. It's presumably for this reason that
monotheistic cultures tend not to have any theatre at all.
Nearer home, it means that theatre is a highly contradictory
business when it plays within the epistemological formation
which Foucault calls Classicism[2] – the positivist, universalist
and empiricist assumptions that underlie the cultural production of the seventeenth and eighteenth centuries. A 'sci-
entific' criterion of truth – that is, one which founds itself on
a unitary law of nature – denies legitimacy to the moment
when the actor puts on his mask, rendering it furtive and
silly. Once all propositions are so organized that they can be
subjected to a single separation of those which are the case
from those which are not, the act of deliberately adopting a
role falls ineluctably into the category of illusion. In other
words, the inauthenticity of the actor's mode of being is a
problematic of the Enlightenment. It's Diderot, in his classic
statement of fascinated mistrust, *Paradoxe sur le comédien*, who
encapsulates the unease in an untranslatable epigram:
'Qu'est-ce donc qu'un grand comédien? Un grand persifleur ... '[3]

  Acting as persiflage, as fooling around, is curiously dramatized in the fourth act climax of *Poetaster*. The poets, and
poetasters, and the ladies they write poems to, organize a
'heavenly banquet' – that is, a dinner at which they all dress

up as appropriate gods and goddesses. The braggart Captain is Mars, the citizen and his upwardly mobile wife Vulcan and Venus, and so on. The fancy dress is the occasion for some fairly obvious repartee, but it's also slightly disturbing, because *Poetaster* itself is a lampoon in which the great literary figures of Augustan Rome are used to portray Jonson and various of his contemporaries. There's thus more than a suspicion that the poets' banquet is Jonson's play *mis en abîme*;[4] in a characteristically circular detail, it's mentioned that the revellers have borrowed some of their Olympian props from an acting company. This correspondence adds a certain piquancy to the way the party is framed. It begins with a formal edict from Jupiter which parodically licenses misrule: all the assembled deities are encouraged to speak foolishly and make love to whoever they like (IV.v.1–49). And it ends when it's interrupted by Caesar himself, whose stiff executive presence reduces the increasingly noisy feast to constraint and humiliation:

Caesar Say, sir, what are you?
Albius I play Vulcan, sir.
Caesar But, what are you, sir?
Albius Your citizen, and jeweller, sir.
Caesar And what are you, dame?
Chloe I play Venus, forsooth.
Caesar I ask not what you play? But, what you are?
Chloe Your citizen, and jeweller's wife, sir.

(IV.vi.19–26)

Caesar's flatly disenchanting distinction jerks the characters out of the irresponsibility afforded them by their divine disguises back into a policed reality where they are held accountable for their actions. The repressive presence of the monarch re-fixes the identities briefly loosened by play; his singleness imposes theirs; in the colourless light of his gaze, the borrowed caduceus, the wine doing duty for nectar, and the rest of the paraphernalia, suddenly look charmless and shameful. The licensing sceptre of the fictional Jupiter is cancelled by the prohibitive sceptre of the actual emperor. Theatre appears, for a moment, as the very negation of social and moral order.

This bizarre and self-destructive piece of theatre is a paradigm for two vital motifs in Jonson's work. The first is the dénouement by unmasking. Brainworm throws off his disguise, Volpone uncases, Wittipol discovers himself. Face shaves. The worthless courtiers of *Cynthia's Revels* are detected beneath the idealized versions of themselves which they have assumed for the masque. Epicoene takes off his wig, thus undeceiving not only everyone else in the play except Dauphine, but also the audience, who of course did know that Epicoene was really (like every other woman on the stage) a boy in disguise, but who thought it was one of the rules of the theatrical transaction that one should suppress this knowledge; and whose faith in stage convention, therefore, has been whimsically abused.

This recurrent image – the physical removal of a disguise in such a context that it at once unravels the intrigue, restores order, and brings the play to an end – is something which further distinguishes Jonson's endings from Shakespeare's. Shakespearean disguise is usually maintained within the scene; and when it is abandoned the wearer's true appearance is either never resumed at all (Viola, Imogen), or else reintroduced in a fresh location, mock-innocently (Portia, Henry V), or ceremonially (Rosalind, Edgar).[5] The jarring, actorish gesture of taking off false hair or borrowed clothes is mostly avoided: the spectators are not to see the inert materiality which overtakes the mask once it becomes an object separated from the body of its wearer. This reverence protects the latent truth of the masks: even if the disguise was at first adopted for purely tactical reasons (and in most cases it isn't that simple), it acquires an air of organic integrity which validates it as a parallel identity. The drama claims a magical space in which Rosalind really was Ganymede, Hero and Hermione really dead; and so implicitly makes the same claim on behalf of itself and of the primary disguises worn by the actors.

In Jonson, by contrast, the mechanics of disguise are at once flaunted and demystified. Inductions and on-stage spectators play double-edged games with the factitiousness of the spectacle; the business of getting hold of costumes required by the intrigue is prosaically stressed; asides point up the gap between mask and face; false identities are assumed unconvincingly and – as in Sir Politic Would-Be's doomed attempt to pass himself off as a tortoise – exploded with brutal laughter. The *indignity* of theatre, the level at which it's a matter of creaking contrivances, false whiskers, funny voices, is harshly insisted on. The text homes in on something flatly derisive in the act of coming out of costume: the message of the brackish nonchalance with which a scar is peeled off, or a foreign gown dropped on a chair, is 'There's no such person – you've been had.' The theatre is not so much a magician, eliciting the secret potentialities of signs, as a buffoon, repeatedly sandbagged by the refusal of things to be anything other than what they ironically are.

The other motif to emerge from the abortive charade in *Poetaster* is related to this rough scepticism about the validity of theatre. It might be called the figure of the absent magistrate. Caesar's sudden arrival is the sudden death of the illusion: the mask is neutralized by his presence, and this shows how his absence – the absence of legitimate authority – was the condition of its virtue all along. This typifies Jonson's theatrical structures: the performance space is cleared by suspending the function of the magistrate. Sejanus flourishes in the power vacuum created by the enigmatic withdrawal of Tiberius, and is annihilated by the eventual reassertion of imperial power. Jeremy the butler blossoms into Captain Face while master is away only to revert on his return. The action of *Bartholomew Fair* begins when the Justice dresses up as a fool and ends when he discovers himself. In the late comedies *The Staple of News* and *The New Inn*, fathers supposed dead or lost are on hand in disguise to watch the conduct of their heirs, which is therefore redefined as a mere trial run when the patriarchs reveal who they are. Everywhere, the theatre opens when the true court closes down, and closes when it opens. It plays the role of the other, not only to the law of nature, but apparently to the law of the realm as well.

Here then is the Jonsonian version of the paradox of the comedian. On the one hand, he is engaged in a uniquely intense and efficacious kind of oratory, holding a mirror up to nature, blending pleasure and instruction, and so helping 'to inform men in the best reason of living' (*Volpone*, Dedication, line 100). As Jonson proudly writes in *Discoveries*, it's the comic poet who most approaches, or even surpasses, the virtues of the orator

> because, in moving the minds of men, and stirring of affections (in which oratory shows, and especially approves her eminence) he chiefly excels. What figure of a body was Lysippus ever able to form with his graver, or Apelles to paint with his pencil, as the comedy to life expresseth so many, and various affections of the mind? There shall the spectator see some, insulting with joy; others, fretting with melancholy ...: no perturbation in common life, but the orator finds an example of it in the scene. (*Discoveries*, 3134–47)

'Comedy to life' comes closer to nature than graphic art because it replaces the effigy with the living mind, and closer than oratory because it completes the effect of words and elocution with what a contemporary character of an actor calls 'a full and significant action of body'.[6] In the service of a true poet, it seems, the theatre is a potent ideological instrument, blending the mimetic and the discursive, 'fortifying moral precepts with examples', and deserving, as Diderot claims to have enjoyed,[7] the magistrate's positive encouragement. But on the other hand, there accompanies this improving and enlightened figure of the actor his vilified, discredited but unexcisable double: the *persifleur*, the clownish and shameless juggler whose capacity for transformations, precisely because the monolinear naturalism of what he is supposed to be doing denies them any conceivable validity, is unlimitedly subversive.

This duality has an interesting social dimension in the ambiguous status of acting as an occupation. Within a social order founded on rank, appearing on the stage for money is a doubtful case: it's not exactly a 'mechanic' pursuit, because it requires too much education, and often involves associating with noble patrons and spectators; yet it isn't a legitimate profession either. As Diderot remarks, parents don't destine their children for the stage, young people are not prepared for it by any recognized education, and it leads to no recognized honours. The life of an actor, he argues, is never chosen, always resorted to; and he concludes that what fits an individual to excel in many different characters is his not having one of his own.[8]

This indeterminacy was particularly extreme for Jacobean actors: servants, as we saw earlier, of the king, yet saved only by that endorsement from the scope of the vagrancy laws; businessmen who in one or two cases became wealthy citizens, yet constantly liable to arbitrary arrest or closure in times of political crisis, public disorder, plague, or moral panic. Their social character thus shares with that of parasites, courtesans and gamblers a certain slipperiness which the characterist Earle expresses in a flurry of verbal equivocations:

> His profession has in it a kind of contradiction, for none is more disliked, and yet none more applauded ... He does not only personate on the stage, but sometimes in the street, for he is masked still in the habit of a gentleman. His parts find him oaths and good words, which he keeps for his use and discourse, and makes shew with them of a fashionable companion ... The waiting-women spectators are over-ears in love with him, and ladies send for him to act in their chambers.[9]

This actor is marginal, eccentric, *demi-mondain*. Diderot briefly imagines an acting profession in which 'gens de bien' might choose to make a career because of its public utility and its honourable place in society. The propriety and self-confidence of such actors, he suggests, would purify the scripts they were called upon to play, and render the theatre an unequivocal force for the improvement of taste and morality.[10] This is to make the theatre ideologically sound by aligning its aesthetics with the values of a hegemonic class; and it suggests, conversely, how the Enlightenment idea of a drama of instruction is (happily) compromised by the contradictory social affiliations of its actual historical medium.

For of course, the application of Diderot to Jonson's predicament can only be taken so far. 'Enlightenment' doesn't define the latter's theatre, but contends within it with other, violently heterogeneous elements. It's true of the stage as of general language that

> At the time of the Renaissance the dual tone of popular speech was waged in a tense struggle against the stabilizing tendencies of the official monotone. For a deeper understanding of the complex and varied manifestations of style of that great epoch, the study of this struggle is exceptionally important and interesting (as is the struggle of the grotesque against the classic canon, the two conflicts being related). This struggle, of course, continued during the following centuries, but it acquired new, complex, and sometimes hidden forms.[11]

Diderot's ironic and subjectivized dialogue might be regarded as one of the hidden forms. The struggle can be watched on Jonson's stage.

When Lovewit returns to his London house after several months' absence, he's surprised to hear from his neighbours about the heterogeneous collection of people who have been frequenting it:

> Ladies and gentlewomen.
> Citizens' wives.
> And knights.
> In coaches.
> Yes, and oyster-women.

Beside other gallants.
                          Sailors' wives.
                                    Tobacco-men.
                          (*The Alchemist*, V.i.3–5)

This miscellaneous clientèle provocatively reflects that of the
theatre itself, and Lovewit's first thought is that his house has
been used for some kind of show. Perhaps his butler has been
exhibiting puppets, or peep-shows such as

> The friar and the nun; or the new motion
> Of the knight's courser, covering the parson's mare;
> The boy of six years old, with the great thing:
> Or't may be, he has the fleas that run at tilt,
> Upon a table, or some dog to dance?
>   (V.i.22–6)

Here, at its most contemptuous, is the humanist's placing of
the popular audience, the beastly multitude who love nothing
that is right and proper. They're credulous rubbernecks, peep-
ing Toms; only the unnecessary multiplication of examples
hints, under the educated dismissal, at a converse fascination
with the grotesque sideshows they flock to.

When Face, now Jeremy the butler, is confronted with the
tales about crowds of visitors, his explanation is different. The
house has been locked and empty all the time. If the neighbours did see all these people,

> They did pass through the doors then,
> Or walls ...
> I should believe my neighbours had seen double
> Through the black-pot, and made these apparitions!
>   (V.ii.25–32)

Actually deserted, the house has been populated by the fig-
ments of drunken hallucination: ''Tis all *deceptio visus*'
(V.iii.62). When the imprisoned Dapper cries out from inside,
Face exclaims desperately, 'Ha! Illusions, some spirit o'the
air' (66). Instead of a freak show, Lovewit's house now
becomes the abode of immaterial spirits.

The point about these two versions of what has been happening is that although the one is a jocular speculation, and the other a bare-faced lie, both come ironically close to the use that really has been made of Lovewit's house during the first four acts. Dapper isn't a spirit of the air, but he is waiting to meet the Faery Queen, allegedly his aunt, who is to give him a magic fly to bring him luck at cards. Unwanted callers at the house have indeed been spoken to by spirits (Dol doing strange voices through a speaking-tube, I.iv.4–5). The naive obscenity of the shows Lovewit imagines is matched by the 'flat bawdry' ('Argument', 11) which is central to the tricksters' operation, and the fraudulence of the fairground marvels echoes the fake wonders of the alchemist's shop – the labyrinth of chemical equipment which is supposed to be bubbling away just off stage, the beautiful sister of a peer driven mad by reading theology, and so on. Like the 'grand balcon' in Genet's play, Face and Subtle's establishment is a brothel which is also a house of illusions:[12] a place where fantastic, phoney images of gratification and power are tailored to the outrageous desires nursed by the paying customers.

Also like Genet's, Jonson's house of illusions is a scandalous reflection on, and of, the theatre in which it's exhibited. Jonson seems to have gone to some lengths to secure this correspondence. The action of the play is continuous except for a possible break between Acts II and III, and two separate plot-lines make it impossible for this gap to be more than about half an hour.[13] Fictional time is as near as possible identical with playing time. Moreover, the date of the action is fixed with unusual precision: it is 1 November, 1610,[14] which chimes curiously with what is known about the play's early stage history. The first recorded performance was in September 1610 in Oxford, where the King's Men were on tour because the London theatres, like Lovewit's house, were closed owing to plague. It's not known whether the play had been presented in London before the close-down in July, but in any case, since the script was new (it wasn't entered in the Stationer's Register until October), it seems obvious that the company would do it in London once the theatres re-opened.

This happened at some time in November, when the coming of colder weather brought the weekly total of plague deaths down to a point where the city authorities regarded it as safe to let crowds assemble again.[15] Lovewit, of course, is supposed to have been keeping an eye on those same statistics, and it's the same drop in mortality that motivates his return to his town house. Thus, even if the date given in the text is not literally that of the London première (and this baroque extreme isn't out of the question), the general circumstances which form the condition of the play's action cunningly coincide with those forming the condition of its performance. To complete the device, the house itself, in and in front of which the entire action takes place, is in the precinct of the Blackfriars, as was the theatre where the play will probably have been performed.

'Lovewit's house', then, as its name neatly hints, is a self-referring image of the theatre. The image is a disgraceful and cynical one, opposed at every level to the aesthetic ideology of classical comedy: the quick-change inventiveness of these performers is not dedicated to the project of combining delight and instruction, or even to the decorously truthful imitation of nature. Rather, it's a definingly *illicit* activity, motivated by petty crime (swindling, prostitution, coining) and exploiting the fantasies of its clients to get away with flagrant violations of probability. *The Alchemist* is Jonson's sharpest realization of the idea of 'that strumpet the stage' (*Underwoods*, xxiii, 34), of actors as the peers, not of the grave orator, but of jugglers and whores. Acting is detached from the official art of rhetoric, and assimilated, in particular, to two unofficial, transgressive codes: that of sex, and that of alchemy.

The first of these is typified by the case of the Spanish grandee. Surly invents this individual in order to undermine the house of illusions, but he rapidly becomes one of its more potent images. Face reacts to Surly's unmasking by assuring Kastril that Surly is an impostor, and that the real Spanish grandee is expected. The young, rich and 'pliant' widow is therefore waiting for him to arrive, and the question arises of who is to adopt the role Surly has unwittingly created. It is offered to Drugger, but only to make him borrow the necessary Spanish costume from an acting company so that Face can be the grandee. In the last act, however, Face abandons this plan when he sees that he can buy Lovewit's forgiveness by handing the widow over to him, thus checkmating Subtle and Dol in a move which he conceals from them until the deal is concluded by pretending that the wedding preparations are still his own. Thus the Spanish grandee takes on a prismatic reality as four different people prepare at different times to 'be' him. Hardly anyone believes that he exists in the normal sense, but the criss-crossing inventions concerning him invest him in a delusive actuality: he is the man who is to marry the widow. This gives the eventual marriage a parodic edge: it's formally the conventional way to end a comedy, but instead of representing a conventional dénouement which restores all the signs to their proper relations, it effects an opportunistic accommodation between authority and illusion. So far from being a Shakespearean vindication of authentic relationship, the wedding is the con-man's masterstroke.

It's hardly an exaggeration to say that this imaginary aristo-crat represents the normal mode of courtship in Jonsonian comedy. Sexuality is constitutively theatrical. Ovid's real interest in the fancy-dress banquet in *Poetaster* is that it affords a chance of seducing Julia; Volpone woos Celia in the guise of a mountebank; Quarlous pursues Dame Purecraft by dress-ing up as the madman Trouble-all. In other cases the false identity is the woman's: when Morose courts Epicoene, as when Mammon courts Dol, he's being imposed upon. The sex in all these relationships is transgressive: the woman is married, or intended to be married, to someone else, or else prostitution is involved. Thus disguise is the recurring form of a rooted opposition of desire and law; eroticism draws people out of their stable rhetorical–legal identities and makes them into comedians, *persifleurs*. Two minor eccentrics exemplify this particularly clearly. In *The New Inn* there's a tailor who, when he's finished a particularly grand dress, has his wife put it on, takes her out to an inn and makes love to her, delivering the dress to the customer the next morning (IV.iii.50–82). He's related to Puntarvolo, the knight in *Every Man Out* who likes to present himself at his own front door as a knight errant, ask for the lord of the castle and, on being informed that he's away from home, be entertained by, and fall in courtly love with, his own wife (II.ii–iii). Both these routines have as their real context respectable monogamous relationships; but the two fantasists are evidently seeking to enliven their marriages with a feeling of adultery. Even when the connection isn't dictated by circumstances, the sexual, the theatrical and the illicit remain intimately interrelated.

Like the images of linguistic proliferation which I discussed in chapter 3, this configuration shifts uneasily in value between inauthenticity and freedom. The playacting husbands inhabit a fools' paradise, and are derisively 'put out of their humours'; the texts in which they appear police the boundaries of their signs with censorious mockery. In the really dynamic comedies – that is, the ones which expose their own semantic ordering to more radical dangers – the pervasive theatricality of sex produces a different and more powerful discourse. Volpone, for instance, attempts to seduce Celia with a vision of sensual delight sustained by unending costume changes. They will act out Ovid's *Metamorphoses*:

> Thou, like Europa now, and I like Jove,
> Then I like Mars, and thou like Erycine,
> So, of the rest, till we have quite run through
> And wearied all the fables of the gods.
> Then will I have thee in more modern forms,
> Attired like some sprightly dame of France,
> Brave Tuscan lady, or proud Spanish beauty ...
> (*Volpone*, III.vii.221–7)

There's no suggestion of resting in any of these roles: the point of the wandering from form to form isn't the naive attraction of this or that disguise in particular, but the multiplication of images itself, the inexhaustible, voluptuous plurality of being. Even the melancholy grandeur of the line about wearying the fables of the gods is not a premonition of satiety; on the contrary, it's a hyperbolic expression of the limitlessness of desire, which devours the entire image repertoire of classical culture and is still hungry. The shifts of the comic intrigue are also drawn into the imagery of metamorphosis: it is Celia's beauty, Volpone assures her, which changed him into a mountebank, which has now transformed him from an invalid into a hot and youthful lover, and which will lead him to contend with Proteus. If the sexual charades of Puntarvolo and the tailor are furtive vacations from the order of truth, Volpone's is a blatant violation of it, breaking out of identity and rioting in difference.

Not that *Volpone* is, even in this perverse sense, a romantic play. Volpone's desires really are criminal; Celia is, it appears, really going to be raped. In other words, the incompatability of order and desire, their refusal to co-exist on the same level of theatrical representation, is a real ideological incoherence. It's one which Jonson attempts to resolve in later plays, with interestingly unsatisfactory results. Just as *The Staple of News* proposes an authoritarian solution to the earlier indeterminacies of the father-and-son story, so *The Devil Is An Ass* and *The New Inn* develop the figure of a positive lover – one, that is, whose courtship is informed by the authorial values on which the text closes as a whole, and who therefore doesn't resort to disguise. In both cases, however, theatricality reasserts itself in other ways. Wittipol's wooing, as we saw, is a set-piece speech occupying the fifteen minutes he has bought from the foolish husband by venturing his cloak; the husband's presence makes it impossible for the lady to reply, so Wittipol crosses the stage and addresses a speech on her behalf to a stand-in for himself. Lovel's situation is yet more formal: he speaks to the lady in a whimsically convened Court of Love. When, consequently, she is moved by his pleading, he interprets her kiss as a part of the courtly game and draws no consolation from it; only by the rearrangement of the identities of half the cast through a tortuous and abstract lost-heir plot is the relationship rescued from unreality. Thus in both courtships, the lover's personal integrity is secured, but the theatrical doublings and illusions are simply displaced from himself to his situation, which is a game. Accepting, within the game, the role of both leading performer and deliberate loser, he makes himself, in every sense, a fool for love. The codes of desire and truth remain mutually inconvertible.

This is specifically a contradiction in the predicament of the wooer – the male lover – and, behind that, in the cultural construction of masculinity which is dominant in Jonson's dramatic writing.

W.J. Ong points out that most male-dominated cultures have puberty rites whose function it is to remove adolescent boys from the feminine environment of childhood and initiate them in a socially constructed code of maleness.[16] Typically, this process involves instruction in a language from which women are excluded; subjection to systematic physical violence; and the inculcation of an ethical system – often sustained by epic literature or folklore – that emphasizes glory, courage and endurance. Ong argues that the grammar school education of the Renaissance was just such a rite of passage, with its exclusive preoccupation with Latin, its addiction to beating, and the unique status it accorded Virgil. The thesis is illuminating and convincing, but also, in a way it doesn't itself acknowledge, rather comical, like a witty debunking. For of course, the classical curriculum itself could hardly accept this neatly functionalist definition of its objectives. As we saw earlier, the claims of Latin were universal ones, its ideological centrality almost unquestionable, its acquisition indistinguishable, officially at least, from that of reason in general. What Ong's insight reveals, therefore, is that classical culture in this institutional context is a contradictory sign, on the one hand representing a universal humanism, but on the other constituting a male difference.

The ethical values predicated by this system reproduce the

same tension. Thus, the 'good man' who is projected as the subject of rhetorical discourse (and dramatized by Jonson in such figures as Crites and Cicero) conforms broadly to a Stoic ideal of personal self-sufficiency: his 'virtue' consists of a control over his emotions, a noble indifference to vicissitude, and a steady perception of the general good, which render him perfect in the Latinate sense – complete, single, free of the dependencies of appetite, affection or weakness. The problem then is not simply that women are perceived as failing to live up to this ideal, but that they're expressly excluded from it. Even the word 'virtue', when applied to a woman, ceases to suggest all those qualities and becomes almost synonymous with 'chastity' – that is, it signifies a concept which is expressible only in terms of the woman's relationship with her husband.[17] She is *supposed* to be dependent, and so can't be supposed to be, in the full sense, virtuous. Within the discourse of classical humanism, therefore, women signify a disturbing negativity – not that the feminine is the *antithesis* of masculine goodness and truth (which would be a fairly easy concept to accommodate) but that it is, as it were, its *obverse*. A lyrical conceit of Jonson's – 'That Women Are But Men's Shadows' – makes the dialectic lightly and powerfully clear:

> At morn, and even, shades are longest;
> At noon, they are or short, or none:
> So men at weakest, they are strongest,
> But grant us perfect, they're not known.
> Say, are not women truly, then,
> Styled but the shadows of us men?

> (*The Forest*, vii.7–12)

Women are a parasitic doubling of the masculine self, strong in its weakness, abolished by its perfection. The logic is that men could fully realize themselves only in a world where women didn't exist. But that ideal is gracefully invalidated by the metaphor of the shadow, which draws attention to the inseparability of the sexes. Masculinity is a differential concept: that is, the concept of femininity is necessary to it and remains a part of it, perpetually subverting its attempts to represent its distinctive values as autonomous and universal.

I've argued in earlier chapters that the complex of values which is at issue here is exceptionally prominent in Jonson's plays. The idealization of the orator, the prestige of classical allusion, the latently sadistic conception of satire as correction, the value-laden oppositions of restraint and incontinence, singleness and multiplicity, sense and chatter – all these themes evince a didactic classicism which no doubt reflects Jonson's own grammar school education, a decisively male initiation in that it detached him permanently from his family and formed his passage to the career of an independent literary producer. The idea of *good discourse* on which his writing is founded is a distinctively 'masculinist' one.

Perhaps surprisingly, this structuring of gender doesn't always entail reductive characterizations of women. There are some quite grossly misogynistic images, notably in the representation of learned women as shallow and presumptuous in *Volpone* and *Epicoene*. But there's also a series of female roles, such as Dol, Grace Wellborn, Mrs Fitzdottrel, and Pru in *The New Inn*, which are largely unmarked by the complementary stereotypes – saint and virago, apathy and hysteria, silence and babble – which the opposition of grammar and femininity tends to produce. The reason is that the femininity of these heroines is not marked in their lines at all. In *Bartholomew Fair*, for example, the assured and relaxed tone of Grace's scenes with Quarlous and Winwife is due to the fact that all three of them speak the *same* correct but colloquial prose. Grace, we could say, is not a 'female character', but a morally conscious (i.e. masculine) individual who finds herself in the position of being a woman. Thus the need to write lines for a female role doesn't in itself have to put the ideology of masculine virtue under strain.

What does put it under strain is sex. It's through sexual desire that women are, in Jonson's suggestive pun, 'known'; and this knowing is also knowledge of the male – that is, of masculinity not as a universal human discourse, but precisely as difference, as imperfection. That manhood which strives to realize itelf by decreeing a world without women is cut across and decentred by a manhood which strives to realize itself *in* women. The monolithic wholeness of the good man – *integer vitae scelerisque purus*[18] – is thrown into division and ambiguity by the sexuality which was its repressed constituent all along; the integral, continent 'classical body' loses its self-sufficient individuality and regains the orifices, protuberances and emissions that assimilate it to transindividual rhythms of proliferation and change.

What this means within the dramatic text is that male sexuality is produced in the form of paranoia: the fantastic apotheoses of Volpone, or the multiple false identities of the Court of Love, or, to return to *The Alchemist*, Face's extraordinary celebration of the sexual reprocessing of the Spanish grandee:

> he shall be brought here, fettered
> With thy fair looks, before he sees thee, and thrown
> In a down-bed, as dark as any dungeon;
> Where thou shalt keep him waking, with thy drum;
> Thy drum, my Dol; thy drum; till he be tame
> As the poor blackbirds were i'the great frost,
> Or bees are with a basin: and so hive him
> I'the swan-skin coverlid, and cambric sheets
> Till he work honey and wax, my little God's-gift.
> (*The Alchemist*, III.iii.41–9)

The Spaniard is of course to be fleeced, and that's the point of the imagery of exploitation; nevertheless, the recherché inuendo, the masochistic sensuality, and the farcical rhythmic and alliterative effects are wildly in excess of the requirements of the situation. Entering these caressing shadows, the masculine self, constructed by grammar and violence, disperses in multiple roles, polysemy, transmutation. It's a kind of enslavement, but also an extreme psychic release: hence the disreputable euphoria of the tone. Structured by this contradition, sexual energy becomes a generator of illusion, a specifically theatrical productivity.

The other such generator in the play is alchemy. The two are linked: when Sir Epicure Mammon sets off in pursuit of Dol Surly remarks:

> Their stone is lechery enough to pay for,
> Without this bait.

(II.iii.265–6)

And they operate in similar ways: alchemy, too, is a process of transmutation; it too, at least on a hostile account, is an expression of illicit desires.

For even in the reductive, coney-catching form it's given in the play, alchemy is more than a simple off-the-peg metaphor for the love of money. In contrast with the monomania which fuels Volpone and Mosca's operation, Face and Subtle's draws on a vivid range of dreams. Drugger, the most modest of their clients, comes for necromantic guidance on the layout of his new shop; Dapper wants a charm to make him a successful gambler; Kastril, who isn't after money even indirectly because he imagines himself to be rich already, wants to be transformed into a fashionable gallant. All three are concerned less with wealth than with success: their tremulous schemes are not calculations of advantage but visions of their own magical transmutation into lucky and enviable individuals. The reference of this dream is to a society without fixed criteria of worth, where the distribution of rewards is frivolous, arbitrary and open to all – in other words, it reflects the individualistic London subculture in which the professional actors themselves moved, using their command of costume and style to make themselves into gentlemen. At one point (II.vi.14–25), Subtle designs a shop sign in which Drugger's name is spelt out as a sort of cabbalistic pictogram. This epitomizes the 'lechery' of the stone: the alchemist will take the formal mark of your individuality and elicit the secret power concealed within it, so that (in the language of a more recent type of magic) you'll see your name in lights.

These are the alchemist's minor works. The stone itself – the elixir which will transmute base metals into gold – is reserved for the Anabaptists and for Sir Epicure Mammon, and in their 'projections' the imagery of personal transformation broadens into a fantastic utopianism. For Tribulation and Ananias, the infinite wealth they anticipate represents infinite power: they will overthrow the Catholic empires and usher in the rule of the Saints. Mammon, the only one of the clients who knows anything about alchemy, shifts excitedly back and forth between its various possibilities. He promises himself a life of monstrous luxury; in itself, this is just a fantasy of being very rich, but he knows that the alchemical work is meant to be a pure and sanctified quest for perfection, so his plans also include, by a mixture of hypocrisy and megalomania, immense philanthropic schemes which will make everyone rich and bring cheating and money-grubbing to an end. But then again, he's aware that the stone has no less miraculous medicinal properties, from which he expects an unlimited allowance of youthfulness and sexual potency; and this merges with the utopian commonwealth to suggest a kind of erotic dictatorship with Mammon himself at its head, turning his rivals into cuckolded millionaires and bejewelled eunuchs. He is, besides, as millenarian as the Anabaptists. Culture is about to end, because it is no more than a catalogue of prefigurations of the imminent discovery:

> the Hesperian garden, Cadmus' story,
> Jove's shower, the boon of Midas, Argus' eyes,
> Boccace his Demogorgon, thousands more,
> All abstract riddles of our stone.

(II.i.101–4)

What connects Mammon's varied ambitions with one another and with those of his fellow-clients is this hunger for the millennium, whether it's personal or global. The Doctor is the man who will move you from the realm of contingency to the realm of desire; in his unseen furnace, the chains confining you to who and what you really are melt away, and your selfhood is renewed, limited in its choice of forms only by the limits of your imagination. Mammon recites for Surly a list of the miserable shifts for money and advantage which will now, with the stone, no longer be necessary; Subtle does the same for Tribulation (II.i.10–22; III.ii.68–97). In a way, these speeches are clearly satiric: the stone is the authorial pretext for an anatomy of abuses. But from another point of view, the motif of 'nor shall you need' signals a miraculous release from the coerciveness of circumstances: from now on, wanting will be enough:

Tribulation We may be temporal lords ourselves, I take it.
Subtle   You may be anything ...

(III.ii.52–3)

This is the seduction of theatre.

Alchemy, after all, is the transformative science *par excellence*, not only in its best-known aim, but in its whole methodology.[19] As a sign system, it works by a constant play of correspondence between different spheres, such that, say, sulphur, earth, matter, blood and woman are interminably turning into one another in the discourse as it slips from one analogue to the next. This principle applies not only to substances, but also to the equipment (thus, the most important vessel is egg-shaped because the production of the stone is thought of as a process of generation, gestation and birth), and to the words which are used (so, 'Mercury' signifies not only the metal and the planet, but also the entire Hermetic tradition, since its semi-legendary founder, Hermes Trismegistus, bears the Greek name of Mercury the god). Alchemy is a theatrical language in the sense that, within it, words and things are not blankly what they are; they are hints, signatures, portents; for the adept who can read the secret symbols of nature, the visible comprehends the invisible, the sublunary the stars. In complete opposition to the monolinear perspicuity proposed by classical humanism and Baconian science, it's a polysemous code, intentionally generating covert meanings, conundrums and commentaries.

It follows that the 'great work' itself is by no means simply a technique for making gold. Rather, the object of the work is the stone itself, which is definable as resurrected matter, substance freed from all corruption and division and consequently immortal. Its capacity to transmute base metal into gold is not, strictly speaking, much more than a test of its purity. The significance of the gold is that if, as the alchemist assumes, all the minerals in the world are essentially differing states of a single universal substance, ranged along a descending scale of perfection, then gold is the purest state which can be found in nature; it's to gold, therefore, that any lower metal may be expected to turn when exposed to the influence of the stone, which is the absolute perfection of matter. That perfection is something to which unaided nature tends and aspires, but which it can never reach: the alchemical intervention which leads to it is thus a case of the familiar Renaissance figure of art the coadjutor, furthering nature and filling out its imperfections by the power of human intellect.

Even from this much simplified outline, it's clear that Sir Epicure's alchemy, massively vulgarized, is not a complete travesty. In his imagination, he walks round London curing the pox and the plague, making old bawds young and beggars rich:

> He will make
> Nature ashamed of her long sleep: when art,
> Who's but a stepdame, shall do more than she,
> In her best love to mankind, ever could.
> If his dream last, he'll turn the age, to gold.
>
> (I.iv.25–9)

Here, as for the serious real-life practitioners, alchemy is not about the local enhancement of some metal, but is the general redemption of nature – not a technique, we could say with hindsight, but technology. Correspondingly, what Subtle is really forging is not just a licence to print money, but a charter to remake the world in accordance with human desire; and so for men – this is the great change which the lesser transformations of Dapper and the others dispersedly reflect – to become gods.

That recalls not only Volpone's offer to Celia, but the serpent's offer to Eve; and certainly Face and Subtle, with their offstage furnace, their shape-shifting, and their semi-nonsensical verbal extravagance, are demonic. The Vice of the Tudor interludes, parodied in *The Devil Is An Ass*, is here directly realized in the terms of Jacobean London, seducing respectable citizens into folly and loss. There had always been, on the religious stage, a structural affinity between diabolism and comic freedom, partly because the context of salvation in Christ renders the devils fundamentally unserious (they aren't going to win in the end), and partly because a devil's utterances, being unconstrained by doctrinal orthodoxy for obvious reasons, clear an irresponsible space between the performer's role and his true identity.[20] But the effect of Jonson's secularization of that opportunity for invention is that the Vice, a bracketed disturbance in the discourse of the moralities, here takes over the action, not only in the negative sense that there is no-one in sight who could be identified as a personified virtue, but positively and dynamically: the seduction initiates, paces and constitutes the comedy itself, just as the house of illusions – 'this seat of falsehood, and this cave of cozenage', as the eventually moralistic Ananias calls it (V.v.115) – is coterminous with the theatre where the comedy plays. We are the ones who have paid to see Lovewit's disreputable peepshows, the friar and the nun, the jousting fleas: our laughter is complicit with the anarchic drives and raging vanities exhibited to us. All fools – but then the show is the fool's hour, the *festa stultorum*.[21] Thus without losing any of its malice, the satire becomes festive, celebrating the devil's fertile brain in the moment of denouncing his falsehood, and subverting the integrity of truth with a scandalous double sign: that-which-is-not-the-case as both an impudent lie and a message from utopia. Alchemy in the play corresponds to that doubleness: it's a parade of antiquated concepts – a lot of old rubbish; but at the same time, in its perspective of man divinized by his mastery of nature, a radiant intimation of the future. As a matter of fact, the radiance is faked. But the authority of fact itself is traversed and disconcerted by the carnivalesque play of deceptions and desires.

Carnival, as Peter Burke points out, is first and foremost a *time*, whose character is defined by its opposition to other times.[22] In the narrow sense it is the festival of flesh – of *carne* – which takes place immediately before the fasting and sexual abstinence of Lent: it is *mardi gras* as opposed to the *jours maigres* that follow. And more generally, all the feast days in which carnivalesque elements are prominent – these include Christmas, Midsummer and, as we shall see, St Bartholomew's Day – take their form from a conscious antithesis with normal time: whereas ordinary days elapse in a closed time, dominated by work rhythms, hierarchies, religious and 'natural' laws which represent themselves as immutable, festival time, precisely because it extends over a fixed period whose predetermined end renders all its arrangements provisional, is open to mutation, laughing inversions, moments of debasement and regeneration. It is, in Bakhtin's words, that 'gay time' which is 'the true hero of every feast, uncrowning the old and crowning the new'.[23] Burke traces that somersaulting movement in the popular imagery of Cockaigne, the topsy-turvy land where the son chastizes the father, the servant gives orders to the master, the poor give alms to the rich, the laity preach to the clergy, the husband carries the baby and the wife carries a gun. It is utopian time: 'Cockaigne is a vision of life as one long Carnival, and Carnival a temporary Cockaigne'.[24]

Against later romanticizations of both the myth and the ritual, it's worth noticing that carnivalesque utopia is not at all a naive wish-fulfilment, a static projection of a world where everything goes right. The game of reversals includes a strong element of nonsense – men are hunted by hares, fish fly, the carnival king rides with his face to the donkey's tail. Even the images of plenty which are central to the festivals of the poor are partly parodic ones: as Jonson knew, the ditches run with cream (*Alchemist*, V.v.76–8) and pigs run about ready roasted looking for someone to eat them (*Bartholomew Fair*, III.ii.66–8). The organizing and disorganizing idea at the centre of the festival is not happiness but inversion, a gay and cruel flight in the face of all existing logic, power, wisdom and good order.

This pervasive spirit of travesty makes carnival, as the whole of Bakhtin's book on Rabelais magnificently demonstrates, the *locus classicus* for 'the dual tone of popular speech'. Carnival discourse is violent and hospitable, dismembering and vivifying, abusive and affirmatory. At the level of origins, this dialogism reflects its pagan affiliations: it's a spring festival of burial and rebirth, whose monarch, like the priest-kings of many ancient cults including Christianity, is both praised and vilified, elevated and executed. Socially, too, carnival is double faced – a wholesale overthrow of ideological norms, but also a holiday observance, occasioned and terminated by the regularity of the ecclesiastical year. (It's perhaps this insouciant combination of total revolt with total incorporation that makes it such a beguiling role-model for literary studies in contemporary academe.) Consistently with that doubleness, carnival is utopian but also in the same breath satiric: its wild violations are not anarchic, but *systematically* negate the power relations which constitute its matrix, producing, as Terry Eagleton remarks, 'in effect, a kind of fiction: a temporary retextualizing of the social formation that exposes its "fictive" foundations.'[25]

In other words, carnival is a kind of comic theatre. Theatrical elements are everywhere essential to the imagery of inversion. The simplest and most universal sign of 'the world turned upside down' is the tumbler, the street performer who turns somersaults or walks on his hands. Mock-combats, mock-trials, mock-executions and travestied religious services and processions must all have had the character of plays. Carnival costume, muddling up the signs distinguishing men from women, clergy from laity, rich from poor, afforded the same kind of holiday from single identity that we've seen pervading Jonsonian comedy; and this freedom had the same links with sexual licence. In the words of an early sixteenth-century poet quoted by Burke,

> *Per fora per vicos it personata libido*
> *Et censore carens subit omnia tecta voluptas*
> (Desire in his mask goes through the squares and streets,
> And in the absence of the censor, Pleasure enters under
> every roof.)[26]

Like Jonson's theatre, this obscene and euphoric visitant flourishes *censore carens*, and like his liars and con-men, he owes his freedom of the city to his mask.

There is, however, an obvious and vital difference, which is that in Jonson the images, however carnivalesque they may be in content, are confined to the theatre. They appear within literary texts which, as we saw, have a powerful if contradictory interest in the distinction between mask and face; and this is in turn presented in a performance space which is unambiguously marked off from the street. Carnival's most formal and fundamental subversion – that of the *real* – is contained within the institution of drama: the semiotic promiscuity of the squares and streets is bracketed by that respectable wedding of sign and referent which is known as representation.

The broad historical terms of this movement of containment are comprehensible. The Jacobean dramatists, after all, were not the contemporaries of Rabelais, and in the seventy-odd years that separate them (exactly the lifetime of Elizabeth I), the situation of popular culture changed fundamentally, in the first phase of the complicated ideological process which Burke calls 'the triumph of Lent'.[27] The scope of carnival contracted under three related attacks: that of the Reformation (and, equally, Counter-reformation) activists who objected to its licentiousness, profanity and vestigial paganism; that of the incipient petty bourgeoisie, who deplored its violence and extravagance; and, most indirectly but probably most decisively, the secular humanist conversion of the ruling class to a code of gentility, refinement and educational élitism, which was one dimension of its integration into the machinery of absolutism and which, by removing its members mentally and literally from the events of the people's year, left popular culture at once more menacingly plebeian and less well protected against suppression than it had been in the early Renaissance. What lies behind these developments, clearly, is that the communal festival of 'the world turned upside down' means something quite new when it's celebrated, not in a stable hierarchical society which fits it into licensed spaces on the calendar, but in the dynamic conditions of emergent class politics. For the egalitarian radicals of the years immediately after Jonson's death, turning the world upside down was not a trope, but a programme. That revolutionary culture drew on the utopianism of politicized puritan groups such as the Anabaptists, and also on the transformative logic of alchemy:[28] Jonson's juxtaposition of the two types of subversion is not simply a piece of satiric opportunism. Under these circumstances, the fictive but actual 'retextualizing of the social formation' in carnival is intolerably ambiguous: there needs, from the official point of view, to be on the one hand the stage, where such rearrangements can be defined as unreal, and on the other the street, where they can be defined as sedition. In the light of these interests, my formulation of the theatricality of carnival should be revised: it's not so much that carnival is a kind of comic theatre as that the comic theatre is a generic stylization of carnival. Nevertheless, containment is not the same as abolition, and the festival forms in Elizabethan theatre, from the carnival court at Eastcheap in *Henry IV* to the nightmare *charivari* in *The Duchess of Malfi*,[29] testify to its contradictory popular affinities.

In this ideological upheaval Jonson, as we've seen in a number of contexts, is explicitly identified with the project of cultural centralization. As a pedagogic and didactic poet he contributed to the formation of an élite humanist culture; as a historically precocious neo-classicist he stood for perspicuity and the separation of genres against the grotesque mode inseparable from carnival; as a conscious 'dramatic poet' he sought to distance his texts from the 'original dung-cart' of popular theatre; and as masque-maker, and poet laureate in all but name, he is arguably the first *official* literary producer in English history. No amount of re-reading could render this cultural trajectory carnivalesque: despite his defence of traditional pastimes against certain kinds of puritan intolerance, he is objectively on the side of 'Lent'. The carnival figures which run through his whole work in the theatre are no less real for that, but they have no access to the fearless and universal gaiety which Bakhtin finds in Rabelais' relations with popular-festive forms. Rather, the carnivalesque in Jonson becomes sly and tense, fraught with danger and perversity; its costumes falsehoods, its inversions crimes, and its promise of liberation anarchic. Cockaigne, repressed, is an *underworld*.

To connect with the logic of this repression, it's helpful to consider another twentieth-century theatrical figure. The most influential modern antagonist of Enlightenment theatre has been Antonin Artaud. In his eyes, the physical necessities and possibilities of the stage had been betrayed by its subordination to the *ratio* of verbal truth. He polemicized against the drama's 'obsession with the defined word that says everything'[30] – that merely elucidatory type of communication which withers the physicality of sonority, breath and gesture, and registers 'only a conclusion'. Against this desiccated theatre of ethical and psychological signifieds, Artaud deploys a Nietzschean fantasia of the stage addressing itself to 'total man'; which does not say things but acts upon its spectators materially, physiologically, oneirically, communicating 'through the skin' and deranging the internal systems of those involved: in short, an alchemical theatre. His most potent symbol for the mode of operation of this 'theatre of cruelty' is the plague.[31]

Taking his cue from stories illustrating the magical and

capricious dissemination of the plague, Artaud regards it as an essentially metaphysical disease, the exteriorization of a 'latent disorder', the explosive release of vital forces violently inimical to the life of societies. The pathology itself is 'absolute and almost abstract'. It's thus an integral part of the plague that an epidemic brings with it an orgiastic collapse of public order. The army and the municipal authorities disappear; the living wander deliriously through streets clogged with the unburied dead:

> The dregs of the population, apparently immunised by their frenzied greed, enter the open houses and pillage riches they know will serve no purpose or profit. And at that moment the theater is born. The theater, i.e., an immediate gratuitousness provoking acts without use or profit.
> The last of the living are in a frenzy: the obedient and virtuous son kills his father; the chaste man performs sodomy upon his neighbors. The lecher becomes pure. The miser throws his gold in handfuls out of the window ... [32]

Lost to (or freed from) all kinds of moral, psychological or purposive stability through the disorganizing power of the pestilence, every form of life passes into its dialectical contrary, becoming that which it had existed by denying. The plague is the vengeful hour of the unconscious; or, in the terms of Artaud's own intolerable spirituality, the time of evil.

This vision of a possible theatre is clearly carnivalesque. The communal, antithetic release of the libidinal, the imagery of inversion, the suspension of the magistrate's authority, the interpenetration of street and private house – all these are unmistakable festival signs. But the gaiety is rendered hectic by the lurid extremism of the impulses which are thus liberated, and by the substitution which represents the collective character of carnival in the image of an epidemic, such that the communication of the disease from one person to another becomes a paranoid metaphor for sociality itself. Here is a carnival darkened and contorted by repression – not a licensed space but, precisely, a forbidden space. This gesture of stretching downward to clutch at the worst is, certainly, of its time (1933): the totalitarian intonations of the ideological speech Artaud is seeking to refuse penetrate even his refusal, transposing his festival from a comic mode into an apocalyptic one. But if his allegory is particular, it isn't merely idiosyncratic.

As I've noted in passing, the theatres of Jacobean London were invariably shut down in time of plague. This was partly in order to prevent large gatherings of possibly infected people, but it was also part of a theological policy of propitiation which included fasting and prayers. In this sense, the ban reflected the logic concisely stated by a preacher in 1577: 'the cause of plague is sinne, if you looke to it well: and the cause of sinne are plays: therefore the cause of plague are plays.'[33] Moreover, this connection seems to have less to do with the plays' content than with the subversiveness of theatre as such. Stephen Gosson argues it in social terms:

> If privat men be suffered to forsake theire calling because they desire to walke gentleman like in sattine & velvet ... proportion is so broken, unitie dissolved, harmony confounded, that the whole body must be dismembred ... God is just, his bow is bent & his arrowe drawn, to send you a plague.[34]

A holiday confusion of ranks – a carnival motif as we saw – leads to the dissolution, the plaguing, of the body politic. The plague itself could also apparently lead in turn to the kind of social breakdown imagined by Artaud:

> in seventeeenth-century London many refused to observe the fasts, and made merry in fields, streets, and taverns ... Thieves wolvishly preyed upon the sick or robbed the dead, and drunkards and whoremongers followed their lusts with the sword of the pestilence hanging over them ... 'Edamus, et bibamus, cras moriemur.'[35]

In this context, it's worth recalling that what makes Lovewit's house available to the alchemist and his associates for what Face calls their 'festival days' (III.iii.54) is the 'sickness' (Argument, 1). The carnivalesque space is cleared by a force which is not a social ritual but rather a social antibody. In less documentary but more decisive fashion, this theatre of disease governs the structure of *Volpone*.

One of Jonson's most direct and positive reproductions of popular theatrical form is Volpone's performance as Scoto of Mantua. Scoto was a real life actor, apparently known in England, not as a seller of medicines, but as a juggler and performer of card tricks: the choice of him as a persona in this scene illustrates how the *ciarlatani* combined the roles of street actor and street apothecary, so that it was hard to say whether their shows were functional sales pitches or free-standing entertainments – whether, that is, to regard their extravagant claims for their medicines as lies or as poetry. The reconciling factor, as Bakhtin argues, is laughter:

> the cries of quacks and druggists operating at the fairs
> belong to the eulogizing genres of folk humor. They too,
> of course, are ambivalent; they too are filled with both
> laughter and irony. They may at any moment show their
> other side; that is, they may be turned into abuses and
> oaths. They too exercise the debasing function, they
> materialize the world, lending it a bodily substance.[36]

The mountebanks were comedians, producing in their patter the carnivalesque rhythms of physical exaltation and degradation. Volpone, as he doesn't fail to observe afterwards, does it well. He begins with grotesque vilification of his rivals: 'those turdy-facy-nasty-paty-lousy fartical rogues ... able, very well, to kill their twenty a week ... meagre starved spirits, who have half-stopped the organs of their minds with earthy oppilations' (*Volpone*, II.ii.57–61). This combines two kinds of festival abuse: the scatological; and the carnival degradation of Lent, the type of everything lean, humourless and constipated. The address then proceeds to the promotion of the miraculous *oglio del Scoto*, with songs and fantastic claims, and finally to the free offer of a secret even more magical than the oil:

> I will, only, tell you; it is the powder that made Venus a goddess (given her by Apollo) that kept her perpetually young, cleared her wrinkles, firmed her gums, filled her skin, coloured her hair; from her, derived to Helen, and at the sack of Troy (unfortunately) lost: till now ... extracted to a quintessence: so that wherever it but touches, in youth it perpetually preserves, in age restores the complexion; seats your teeth, did they dance like virginal jacks, firm as a wall. (II.ii.216–27)

The grotesqueness of this eulogy exemplifies the dual tone of the genre. The legendary beauties dignify the powder, but equally the powder, together with the reductive anatomy of the goddess and the surreal image of the dancing teeth, undermines the dignity of the legend. The parodic construction of the vision of eternal health keeps farcically in view the disease and decay which are its stimulus, materializing the world.

The fidelity and comic energy with which Jonson has produced this satiric-panegyric popular accent is itself reason to doubt the reading which accepts Peregrine's 'common-sense' scepticism as exhaustively authorial. Scoto on his mountebank's stage is presenting a play within a play, as Corvino recognizes when he objects to being cast as Pantalone in his *commedia* scenario. Two types of theatre confront one another on the stage; and since the plot neatly wrongfoots Peregrine (less naive than Sir Politic, he is no less wrong about what 'Scoto' is actually up to), his flat insistence on that-which-is-the-case is by no means conclusive. Although, or because, Scoto's act is a double falsehood – not only is his powder not really the elixir of life, but also he isn't really Scoto – it's the broadest and frankest statement of the carnival themes that run through Volpone's entire role.

Firstly, the comic debasing of classical legend is characteristic of the entertainments presented by Volpone's fairground children, the dwarf, the eunuch and the fool. Nano's song in the character of Scoto's assistant Zan Fritada (II.ii.112–23) invokes the names of Hippocrates, Galen and Paracelsus with insulting familiarity; similarly, in a close parallel to the mock-heroic descent of the elixir, the first of the trio's sketches (I.ii.1–81) traces the transmigrations of Androgyno's soul from Apollo through various heroes, animals and satirical types, finally to come happily to rest in the body of a fool. Not only does the bathetic destination of the long journey discredit its illustrious early stages, but also the style in which the successive worthies are described (Menelaus is 'the cuckold of Sparta', Pythagoras himself a 'juggler', and so on) cuts their historic pretensions down to the scale of street farce. It's a fool's pageant, a laughing world history of clowns and punks.

Secondly, Volpone's temporary role as a theatrical doctor is an inverted variant of his permanent role as a theatrical invalid, in which the exigencies of the plot are constantly killing him and bringing him back to life. Act I lays down the basic rhythm, as Volpone alternates between sickness and the delighted vitality with which he 'leaps from his couch'. The contraries feed on each other: as Volpone's pleasure and excitement rise, he becomes more and more ill; merely weak for the first visitor, he is paralysed for the second and virtually dead for the third, before launching himself into the pursuit of Corvino's wife. This raises him up as Scoto; Corvino's intervention returns him to his sickbed, from which he is miraculously revived by Celia's arrival. Baulked once again, he relapses, and appears in court in Act IV unable to speak or move; off the top of the success of this manoeuvre he embarks on the ploy of being dead; there follows the contest with Mosca – Volpone struggling to come back to life, Mosca to keep him dead – with the eventual result that he delivers himself over to judgement and is resurrected and 'mortified' for the last time. One of the motifs linking the contrasting phases is that of <u>incontinence:</u> Volpone's disease expresses itself in disgusting discharges, so that his eyes 'flow with slime,/Like two frog-pits', his cheeks resemble 'an old smoked wall, on which the rain/Ran down in streaks', and his nose 'is like a common sewer, still running' (I.v.57–65); while the healthy Volpone is subject to comparable outbursts, as Mosca urges him, in an appropriately medical metaphor, 'Contain/Your flux of laughter' (I.iv.133–4), and his lust for Celia is Cupid penetrating his body:

> Where now he flings about his burning heat,
> As in a furnace, an ambitious fire,
> Whose vent is stopped. The fight is all within me.
> I cannot live, except thou help me, Mosca;
> My liver melts ...
>
> (II.iv.5–9)

Both the symptoms of the disease and the actions of the comic role are, in Artaud's expression, the exteriorization of a latent disorder, a pathological breaking out. It's not merely impressionistic to say that the pace of the farce is feverish: its rhythms are those of the violent dissolution and regeneration of the carnivalesque body.

Its frenzy is, moreover, communicative. Under its influence, the lawyer commits perjury, the aged father disinherits his virtuous son, the jealous husband forces his wife to sleep with another man, the knight's wife kisses a hideous oily face, the slave becomes a magnifico and the master a common sergeant – the plot rivals Artaud's catalogue of pestilential reversals. The money-grubbing suitors become devotees of the imaginary: Voltore reviews his chances 'And then concludes, there's naught impossible' (I.ii.108); Corbaccio, more rotten with disease than Volpone can pretend to be, 'hopes he may/With charms, like Aeson, have his youth restored' (I.iv.155–6), drawing a delusive health from Volpone's delusive sickness. Even Celia expresses her purity in masochistic fantasies of disease:

                                          Rub these hands
With what may cause an eating leprosy,
E'en to my bones and marrow: anything
That may disfavour me, save in my honour.
                                          (III.vii.253–6)

By degrees, all these dreams are worked into a many-layered
tissue of illusions so complicated that it's almost impossible
to remember who is lying, who is deceived, and what the
truth is anyway. Fantasy invades the court house where truth
and error are supposed to be disentangled: when Voltore
makes the mistake of revealing some of the facts, a pantomime
of dispossession drives the devil out of him in the shape of a
blue toad that flies out of his mouth (V.xii.24–35). Volpone's
protean and abstract malady is a theatre which generates
'incredible images which give freedom of the city and of
existence to acts which are by nature hostile to the life of
societies'.[37] Only Volpone's unmasking, revealing himself as
alive and well, brings the collective delirium to an end and
restores a joyless and punitive – a Lenten – order.

   Thus Volpone's sickness is a radically divided sign. Read
as representation, it depicts a lie; a criminal stratagem whose
success signifies only the folly and greed of those who are
taken in by it. In this frame, Volpone and Mosca's self-
congratulation, for instance, after their Act IV *coup* is gloating,
as sordid and immoral as the trickery it celebrates:

Volpone   Exquisite Mosca!

Mosca   Was it not carried learnedly?

Volpone   And stoutly.
          Good wits are greatest in extremities.
Mosca   It were a folly beyond thought to trust
          Any grand act unto a cowardly spirit ...
                                 We must here be fixed;
          Here we must rest; this is our masterpiece:
          We cannot think to go beyond this.

Volpone	True,
	Thou'st played thy prize, my precious Mosca.
Mosca	Nay, sir,
	To gull the court –
Volpone	And quite divert the torrent,
	Upon the innocent.
Mosca	Yes, and to make
	So rare a music out of discords –
Volpone	Right.

(V.ii.4–18)

The elevated humanist concepts – learning, wit, greatness of spirit, *concordia discors* – are in this reading undeserved: the comedy (which is therefore satiric) consists of the gap between the high sententious tone and the base actuality. Read as performance, on the other hand, Volpone's sickness is a kind of carnival: a celebration, against the rigid categories of official culture and legality which the first reading takes for granted, of the ceaselessly dying and renewing body, its devouring and discharging laughter, and the invincible resourcefulness with which it provokes fresh transformations. In this context, the parodic vaunting of the tricksters doesn't so much enforce as undermine the authoritarian barrier between what is and what could be: they're artists, trans-muters of nature, concluding there's naught impossible. And if the authorially controlled plot endorses the ethical con-demnation of lying and cheating, the *show* is riding shame-lessly on the flight in the face of truth: that is, the moralism of the text is dialogized by its complicity with its own staging.

What holds the role together across the division is a simple fact about acting: that on the stage there is no necessary difference between the symptoms of a 'real' disease and those of a simulated one. The one is worth the other – carrying the same meanings and producing the same effects. Acting the text – or, better, *playing* it – randomizes the relationship of verbal or visual signs to their expected referents: this dis-location is both a corrupting inauthenticity (as it is for Gosson) and a euphoric liberation of the signifier. In other words, the figure which brings the festival and the lie into contradictory unity is that of the actor – the regal vagabond, the magician-buffoon. As actors themselves realize, it's Jonson's definitive theatre role:[38] Volpone *is* an actor, not just in the sense that he changes roles a lot, but also in his unstable mixture of magnificence and tat, godlike humour and abjectly unconvincing expedients, poetic mastery and childish vanity.

However, the tension between the two theatres of *Volpone* doesn't have the static equilibrium of a paradox. Two related factors drain the materiality from the festival imagery and alter its meanings. One is the privatization of the action: concentrated on Volpone's jewelled and claustral sickroom, from which he can escape to the marketplace only by adopting a second tier of disguise, the carnival is secretive, anti-social, celebrated in darkened rooms and seductive whispers. Just as the institution of theatre cuts the spectacle off from the street, so the comedy of Volpone's diseases is cut off from the flamboyant public healing of Scoto. The actor is denied historical reality. Secondly, there is Volpone's infertility. His childlessness is the condition of the whole plot, and the private entertainers who are said to be his illegitimate offspring are themselves theatrical and sterile, gaudy frivolous children who can grow old but not grow up. His regenerative potency, his carnality, is thus confined to himself: it has the magical polymorphism, but not the universality, of carnival. Both of these blocks upon the fluidity of the carnivalesque hero work to isolate him from his popular–festive milieu; they are both traces of the classical predicament of the actor as alienated and unreal, able to imitate but not connect, seduce but not procreate; together they limit the productivity of the image. Or rather, they don't so much limit as abstract it. For what breeds instead, in Volpone's voluptuous and lonely bed, is money.

Something always escapes, though. There's a moment in *Bartholomew Fair* when Knockem, the horse-dealer and pimp, buys Trouble-all a drink. Trouble-all won't accept it without a warrant from Justice Overdo, so Knockem gets a piece of paper, signs it 'Adam Overdo' and hands it over with the beer (IV.vi.1–13). Then the play goes on to something else. What's remarkable about this understated incident is its insouciance about reality and illusion. Trouble-all is crazy (he doesn't really need Justice Overdo's warrant) and Knockem is fooling him (it isn't really Overdo's signature); but because neither of them has the slightest interest in maintaining the categories of sanity and authenticity, Trouble-all gets his drink. There's a tacit contrast with the real Overdo. The Justice is a conscientious man who, as soon as he understands that he is unwittingly reponsible for Trouble-all's distressing condition, is determined to make amends; his attempts to do him good, however, are completely ineffectual. Knockem, an unscrupulous, aggressive and rather inane individual, has no motive for his act of kindness, which is presented without comment. The funny and inconsequential little scene has no ethical or juridical validity – only the beer is real; whereas with Overdo's philanthropy it's the other way round.

The lightness and freedom of the dramatic mode in which a moment like this is possible are almost bewildering after the tension and frenzy of the other two great comedies. *Bartholomew Fair*, after all, has recognizably the same comic structure. It shows eleven respectable citizens, various in rank and character, who visit the Fair and lose themselves there, through disguise, through being gulled, or through the familiar Jonsonian figure of wooing as a game. The Fair is evidently an equivalent of the alchemist's shop or Volpone's sick-room: a space where stable identities dissolve in ambivalently proliferating forms of desire and which, in its asymmetrical combination of utopianism and deception, is the theatre's own self-reflected image. But if the themes seem continuous in some respects, the apparently arbitrary disappearance of the problem of validity transforms the tone; in particular, the popular–festive note, which I've described as repressed and distorted in the other plays, here seems to be struck directly. This can be illustrated by picking out some of the *stories* that crowd the text.

Two zealous puritans are led to the Fair by a pregnant woman's pretended craving for pork. This motivation combines two carnivalesque motifs: the affirmation of the body against the denying spirit, and the pork itself, which is the carnival food *par excellence*. They arrive at the booth of the enormously fat pig-woman Ursula, who is, as one of them remarks, 'the world, as being in the Fair; the devil, as being in the fire; and the flesh, as being herself' (III.vi.32–3). She is also liquid, awash with beer and sweat: 'I am all fire and fat, Nightingale, I shall e'en melt away ... I do water the ground in knots, as I go, like a great garden-pot' (II.ii.46–9). Here, it seems, is the gay popular celebration of carnality which Volpone represented in criminalized and self-divided form. Her torrential, materializing abuse is, with startling directness, Carnival's vilification of Lent:

> Aye, aye, gamesters, mock a plain plump soft wench o' the suburbs, do, because she's juicy and wholesome: you must ha' your thin pinched ware, pent up i' the compass of a dog-collar (or 'twill not do) that looks like a long laced conger, set upright, and a green feather, like fennel, i' the jowl on't. (II.v.74–8)

Despite their disapproval, the devotees of the spirit are lured under her pig's-head sign by the direct physical effect of the scent of roasting pig; once in the tent, they consume a gigantic meal of pork and bottle-ale. They wander the Fair under its influence in an increasingly excited state, and eventually, in a sort of profane redemption, are separately converted to worldliness, one through her sudden passion for a madman, and the other through a disputation with a puppet called Dionysius, which the puppet wins by taking down its trousers. Similarly the Justice, dressed in motley, hunts 'enormities' among the booths like an undignified parody of the Duke in *Measure for Measure*. He misunderstands everything, is beaten and put in the stocks, and is offered his own wife for a shilling. In the famously genial conclusion, he is successfully urged to recall that his name is Adam, 'flesh and blood', and invite everyone to supper. His intended dénouement, a solemn distribution of just rewards and punishments, turns into a 'banquet for all the world'. Legal and religious authority has been routed by the overturning energy of food, drink, sex and laughter. Thus it appears that the play not only finds a carnivalesque language free of the suppressions and displacements I've traced in the other texts, but also that it's allowed to keep its authority right to the end: Lent never comes.

I have told these stories in somewhat superficial style: no doubt a different kind of commentary could 'dig deeper'. But then the tone of buoyancy I'm trying to identify is found, precisely, on the surface of the text; not implicit, but patent, in the crude gestures and cheerful, debunking materialism. That's the point about Trouble-all's beer taking priority over its meaning: the rejection of legality and piety is also a rejection of the symbolic.

What are the conditions of this anomalous freedom? Part of the answer to this is to be found in the play's peculiar theatrical construction.

As I mentioned, there are eleven visitors to the Fair. On the other side, there are sixteen named persons who are part of the Fair in one way or another. This is a large enough cast to represent a crowd – a point whose significance I'll return to – but Jonson organizes it into coherent groups. The visitors are essentially two families: Overdo's, consisting of himself, his wife, his ward, and his wife's brother with his servant; and the Littlewits, husband and wife, with the wife's mother and godfather, the mother's suitor and his friend. The two groups are linked, initially, by the fact that it's Littlewit who issues the licence for the marriage which is shortly to take place within the Overdo group, between Grace and Cokes. That's to say, the types of relationship which connect the visitors with one another are legal and permanent in character: kinship, marriage, service. Among the Fair people the main grouping centres on Ursula. As a stallholder she is neighbour to Leatherhead and Joan Trash; as a pigwoman she employs the tapster Mooncalf; as a bawd she provides home base for the pimps Knockem and Whit; and as a fence she deals with the purse-cutting team of Nightingale and Edgeworth. No-one of any importance is outside this system of relationships except the three officers of the watch and the solitary and ubiquitous Trouble-all. Its coherence is equal to that of the visitors' group, but opposite in character: there are no family relationships, just atomic individuals – 'masterless men' – linked by business arrangements. Corresponding to the opposed social formations there's a subtle opposition of dramatic modes. It's the visitors who, as it were, lead the dramatic focus around the Fair; the play is their stories; the Fair people are, roughly speaking, what happens to the visitors. If we imagine the scenes as extracts from the characters' longer and fuller day (as the high frequency of exits and entrances invites us to do), then we could say that in the visitors' case the selection is made with them in mind, whereas for the Fair people the basis for the selection is external to them. Even in a scene such as the singing of the ballad of the cutpurse, although Nightingale and Edgeworth are clearly the leading actors, it's also clear that they're working a device they've used many times before: what makes it an event is its singleness in the experience of the victim, Cokes, and the delighted spectators, Winwife and Quarlous. The visitors' consciousness is *structuring*; that of the Fair people is subordinate to the structure, but also, through that subordination, *at liberty* – as they have no dramaturgic responsibilities, their attitude to the plot is free-and-easy.

The essential overall movement of the action is the dissolution of the visitors' group in the element of the Fair. This is total: by the beginning of the last act every visitor has lost touch with the people he or she came with. About half of them have formed new sub-groups across the Overdo–Littlewit divide; the other half are wandering about by themselves. The play thus stages a reversal in the relations between its contrasting modes: the subordinate consciousness of the atomized society invades and disintegrates the structuring consciousness of the legal and domestic one; the context, so to speak, swamps the text.

It's this profound structural joke which produces the impression that the play is sprawling and episodic. Nothing could be further from the truth. As an instance of the intricate economy of the plotting, take Quarlous' marriage to Dame Purecraft. It comes about because he dresses up as Trouble-all: his reason for doing that is to find out which name the madman marked in Grace's book, but the disguise also has two inadvertent effects. One is that Purecraft's affection for Trouble-all unwittingly transfers to him, and the other is that he can use Overdo's desire to do Trouble-all a good turn to get his signature for a marriage licence. Why is Purecraft attracted to the madman? It's partly because his obsession with Overdo's warrant leads him to harass the watch, and this has twice led to Busy's release from the stocks, causing her to regard him as a form of heavenly intervention. And how did Trouble-all's plight come to Overdo's attention? Because he was in the stocks too when Trouble-all was harassing the watch, and he was naturally interested in someone who kept repeating his own name. Thus the madman disguise, and behind it the farcical scene around the stocks, unsuspectingly contain the two necessary conditions for Quarlous' eventual marriage. But why does he want to marry Purecraft anyway? Because his hopes of Grace have been disappointed – as he has just learned by disguising himself as Trouble-all.

This is construction as ingenious as Jonson's more conspicuous virtuosity in *Volpone* and *The Alchemist*. Yet there's something dislocating about it: hence the odd combination of tight plotting with the impression of plotlessness. On the one hand, the crossing over of plot-lines makes a mockery of relationship; the people whose actions dictate Quarlous' destiny are not even conscious of his existence; the remoteness of the causation is absurd. And conversely, the disguise is overloaded with consequences: a sort of structural polysemy multiplies the facets of the action beyond the actor's intention, crating an atmosphere in which, whenever anyone starts anything, it's liable to get out of hand.

Socially, the ground of this contradictory effect of interconnectedness and fragmentation is the fairground itself. Its concentration of diverse lives in a finite time and space provides a sharply outlined image of the heterogenous and horizonless unity of the crowd. The paradoxical openness of the dramatic texture comes about because when the highly organized interrelationships are produced in the linear sequence of playing time, the result is an apparently endless series of non-relational contiguities: it's always possible for any of the characters to walk out of her own story into someone else's by simply moving on to the next booth. The theatrical mechanics of this representation (for of course the play isn't really a fair, despite a sophisticated prefatory pretence that it is) can be exemplified by a closer look at one act. To make the relations clearer, I have set out the relevant scenes in schematic form; see table opposite. (Under 'Events' I've noted only things which are relevant to my argument; this is not a summary of the action. Action normally goes straight on from one scene into the next: a continuous line marks a necessary change of scene, and the broken line a possible one.)

In the terms of representational theatre, there are two striking anomalies here. One is the length of time it takes Win to relieve herself. She is in Ursula's booth for about half an hour in playing time, and when she comes out, Edgeworth has committed two more robberies, and the vapours game has come and gone right in front of the entrance. It's as if Jonson is writing in simultaneous scenes – as if the three-quarters of an hour or so occupied by Act IV in the theatre shows, as it were, the events of the *same* period of twenty-five minutes in two different parts of the Fair. But I doubt whether such a convention would be readable by an audience; and in any case, it doesn't strictly work, because the different scenes

Scene	Location	Events
III. vi. (1–122)	Before Ursula's booth (see line 1)	Busy arrested (100) Win goes into Ursula's to urinate (117)
IV. i. (1–97)	The stocks (30)	Busy brought in (77)
IV. ii. (1–97)	(No evidence)	Edgeworth steals Cokes' cloak
IV. iii. (1–116)	Behind Ursula's booth (115)	Edgeworth reports on vapours game and invites Quarlous to come and see it (98–116)
IV. iv. (1–202)	Before Ursula's booth (173–4, 200)	Edgeworth and Quarlous watch the game (from line 18) Wasp arrested (153)
IV. v. (1–94)	The same	Littlewits come out of Ursula's (1) John leaves for the puppetshow (8)
IV. vi. (1–157)	The same (16) The stocks (42–145)	Wasp put in the stocks (47)
V. i. (1–20)	The puppet-show booth (1)	
V. ii. (1–119)	The same (118)	
V. iii. (1–114)	The same	Littlewit arrives (12)
V. iv. (1–334)	The same	Littlewit leaves to find Win (12) Win arrives with Edgeworth (19)

don't have wholly independent casts – there's always somebody shifting from one story into another. Rather, the point
is that the play doesn't have a unified time-scale: there's no
authoritative 'day' to which all the separated trajectories of
the characters conform (even the watch don't know what time

it is – see III.i.14–27), but a ramshackle ensemble of different times that chime only when people become involved in the same scene. In this case, Littlewit time, so to speak, is slower than Edgeworth time – a point which is rather confirmed when Win, having been left in the hands of the pimps while her husband goes and sees to his puppets, is persuaded to go on the game, changes her clothes, and arrives with her new protectors at the puppet show only a few minutes after him. She has crossed over from one time-scale to another.

Such indeterminacy is made easier by the peculiar handling of location. During our sequence, both Busy and Wasp are arrested outside Ursula's booth in separate incidents. Both are shown leaving the stage under guard, and then, a short and consistent time afterwards, being put in the stocks. It seems clear that the booth and the stocks are supposed to be in different parts of the Fair, a short walk apart. But the action of IV.iv–vi is continuous: Wasp's re-entrance in scene vi ought to be an arrival at the very spot from which he was removed in scene iv. He is stocked in front of Ursula's. This makes no sense: evidently the stage is not representing place in this static and specific manner at all. Locations can change with no break in the action; there are some scenes which take place nowhere in particular. This freedom of convention is also working, in a less cut and dried fashion, in IV.i–ii: scene ii runs on from a scene which takes place around the stocks – a most unlikely place for Edgeworth to choose for a rather elaborate theft. The action has moved, at an indeterminate point, to somewhere else; and the location remains unspecific until the end of scene iii, when Quarlous and Edgeworth find themselves at the back of Ursula's.

What this means for practical staging is almost certainly that Acts II–IV, at least, are to be played on a permanent 'Fair' set with the stocks, the pig sign, and several booths visible all the time. (We know that real booths, or at least their facades, were erected on stage for the first performance;[39] and certainly the stocks have to be practicable.) As in modern touring productions of 'epic' plays with a large number of scenes, the actors use a central all-purpose playing area, homing in as necessary on whatever bit of scenery the action makes temporarily relevant. The stage image implied by these deductions is an interestingly ambiguous one. On the one hand, it was possible for the stage Fair to be much more like the real thing than was usual in Jacobean theatre: Jonson has, so to speak, evaded his own neo-classical dissatisfaction with the unnaturalness of theatre by choosing an object of representation which, in its theatricality, its temporary canvas-and-paint mode of existence, is uniquely amenable to direct reproduction on the stage. On the other hand, the simultaneous presence on the stage of different 'houses', between which the action moves in conventional violation of the constraints of time and space, recalls the cosmic space of the emblematic theatre with its 'mansions'[40] – there's even something emblematic in the nonrealistic juxtaposition of the pig (carnival) and the stocks (law).

In other words, *Bartholomew Fair* is a theatrical hybrid. Its open and fluid treatment of time and space is interrupted by moments of great representational exactness. Thus, if the 'scene change' within IV.vi is invisible and stylized, that between IV.iii and iv is very deliberate and naturalistic; or again, the time lag in Littlewit's toing and froing between the puppets and his wife seems irrelevant until the pointed and farcical moment in V.iv when he misses her by seconds. Combinations of people and events which require a unified conception of time and location alternate with combinations which make it impossible. In this way the heteroglossia of the represented society, the reciprocally competing and estranging co-existence within it of different speech types, different readings of time and place, different social practices and projects, permeates the representation. The plural, disproportioning crowd, which we saw attaining the status of a *discursive* subject in the letter from *Every Man In* discussed at the beginning of chapter 3, here becomes a *dramatic* subject: the theatrical language as a whole adopts the zig-zag movement of the *flâneur*.

This is ironic in the Socratic sense – it's extremely hard to say whether Jonson is being cunning or stupid. For while formally the play observes the 'unities' with pedantic rigour, it does so in a way that defeats them. The unity of time is not only strict, but conspicuous because the story is that of a day out – but then just that prominence of the device emphasizes that the simultaneity of the different stories, like that of strangers on a train, is abstract and forced; the times of diverse subjects don't integrate, but interfere, with one another. Unity of place is similarly flaunted: the whole action takes place in London, and everything after Act I in the same few hundred square yards. But then the detailed action, as we've partly seen, turns systematically on the experience of getting lost: the multiple separation of companions, and coinciding of strangers, shatters the site into fragments and problematizes exactly that relationship between theatrical and fictive space which the unity of place is supposed to make easy. And unity of action, procured by a vast labour of interconnected plotting, amounts in effect to a ramified ironic commentary on the arbitrariness of outcomes: Winwife's meeting Grace is a by-product of his pursuit of Purecraft; Overdo's attempt to save Edgeworth from bad company draws the crowd which enables the latter to pick pockets in safety. The forcible unification of the action serves to give the highest definition to the image of its multiplicity.

Thus on all three counts, formal unity turns into a mechanism for the production of difference. The dramatic image is plural and horizonless, not because Jonson deviates from the principles which are meant to keep it one and entire, but because he carries their application to an extreme where they parody themselves and subvert the ideal of naturalness from within – in other words, unity is not violated, but deconstructed. Hence the strange disappearance of the preoccupation with the falseness of the theatre: it's not possible to have one uniquely true representation of the world when there is no unified dramatic consciousness in which to represent it – and so the idea of *false* representation loses its edge.

For what had contorted the other plays was the contradiction between the dramatist's intention – to depict the world as it is – and the means at his disposal – disguise, pretence, unreality. The theatre was split down the middle by the radical ambiguity of the word 'show'. In *Bartholomew Fair*, by a happy coincidence, that rift is mended because the depicted world is itself a show – in the sense, certainly, that a fair is a collection of 'sights' exhibited to spectators, but more structurally in the sense that in the Fair's estranging network of intercutting personal trajectories, everyone *is* such an exhibit for everyone else. Everyone is detached from the institutional fixities which guarantee his 'real self'; every identity is made over to the transformative fluidity of the crowd. Thus the play's representative function ceases to pull against its material presence in the theatre; the performance itself resembles what it denotes.

This equivalence is acted out as comedy in the conclusion of the play. The process of fragmentation is more or less complete by the end of Act IV; Act V is a contrary movement which reassembles the cast bit by bit until everyone is on the stage together. The agency of this summons is the puppet show: the persons of the play are brought together as an *audience*. In conferring this unity on them, though, the show doesn't in the least undo the confusions and divisions of the day: it just draws them physically into the one room, where the dynamic diversity of their experience is held in the suspension of their common attention to the performance. This stage audience is thus a uniquely concrete and historical one: it's more than a microcosm of society – in the terms of the larger play it *is* society; the human trace of everything that has happened. The show plays to all the world.

What they see falls into three phases. In the first, the scripted puppet play, the legend of Hero and Leander is performed in the language of London tapsters and whores, full of grotesque puns and Billingsgate abuse. The show here reflects the world of its audience (the world of the Fair) and at the same time discrowns and materializes the world of myth. Like Jonson's comical satires, it's a fiction which parodically discredits itself. The second phase is Busy's disputation with one of the puppets. Now the parody extends outwards into the auditorium: on the one hand, the puppet departs from the script and starts behaving as if it were real; on the other hand Busy, as the ludicrous encounter reduces his debating points to prattle, turns into a puppet. The third phase of the show completes this interpenetration of stage and auditorium, as Overdo's attempt to replace the dual tones of the parodies with a grandiosely monologic oratorical theatre – 'look upon me, O London! And see me, O Smithfield; the example of Justice, and Mirror of Magistrates' (V.vi.29–30) – is itself rendered parodic, not only by its own bathos, but by the anarchic irruption of accidents undermining the sovereignty of his discourse. Quarlous coaxing his new bride, Littlewit searching feebly for his wife, Trouble-all with Ursula pursuing him for her pan, the discovery of Win and Mrs Overdo under the whores' masks: the opaque particularity of the Fair is unleashed from every side, making a nonsense of Overdo's claim to be revealing all by the transparency of his single utterance. By this time the scope of the puppet stage has broadened out until it's coterminous with the stage of the playhouse: the stage audience is watching the conclusion of *Bartholomew Fair*.

This is an entertaining reversal of the banquet scene in *Poetaster*. Again a piece of foolish play-acting is interrupted by the magistrate, but this time the effect is not to bring the revels to an end by exposing the gap between reality and pretence; instead, that gap is closed up altogether and the magistrate becomes part of the show. State power has lost its absolute capacity to determine what is really the case and what is not. What makes the difference is the presence of the audience. Caesar broke in upon a private charade; his intervention had the character of indisputable public reality discovering and shaming individual deviation. The performance was a falsehood because it was abstracted from any material, public context; an exactly corresponding abstraction permitted the magistrate to stand for society as a whole. Overdo lays claim to the same monologic authority, but the heteroglossia of the crowd puts his word in an environment, decentring it, objectifying it, robbing it of its transcendence by making it part of the spectacle. Like Morose, Overdo finds that the attempt to impose an authoritarian fixity on the dialogic productivity of social interaction rebounds on himself: whereas Caesar (and Lovewit, and the judges in *Volpone*) brings the real world disenchantingly to bear on a house of illusions, Overdo, entangled in the unlimited illusions of the open Fair, accepts that his judicial authority is one more such illusion and invites the whole show into *his* house. The last line of Jonson's play (spoken by Cokes, the fool who falls for every illusion) is 'bring the actors along, we'll ha' the rest of the play at home.'

Subit omnia tecta voluptas. Bartholomew Fair is able to stage the imagery of carnival because it reproduces its fundamental condition: that the subject of the discourse is collective; neither an official nor a deviant individual, but the whole body of the people. Instead of gazing back at the real world across an epistemological barrier, fiction realizes itself as a form of social production – not representation, but play. What Knockem was doing, after all, when he pretended to authorize Trouble-all's drink, was neither endorsing nor rejecting the madman's requirement, but accepting it as the rule of a *game*. A game is imaginary (the players' moves within it neither bind nor are bound by their actions and identities outside it) but not unreal (it's something they are really doing, not merely pretending to do): what dissolves that apparent paradox is its interpersonal character – it can't be the work of an author, but is a transaction between several players. It's fiction lived. The universal game of carnival, then, is a fiction entered upon by an entire society; and it's in the terms of such a fiction that Busy is confuted by the puppet, and the Smithfield Mirror of Magistrates uncrowned. The eventual *raisonneur* is the 'gamester' Quarlous.

Thus the persistent opposition of theatre and authority is

for once resolved by the unconditional surrender of the latter. The theatre's victory is released from its attendant plagues and demons by its reconnection with popular culture: thieves, whores, con-men and fools are welcomed without distinction into the Justice's house in the general amnesty of carnival. It was a unique materialization: Jonson's later comedies don't repeat it, and even *Bartholomew Fair* itself, after its double première, doesn't appear to have been revived until the Restoration.[41] This tone of a single event is preserved in the Induction, in which a scrivener comes on and reads out a contract, concluded at the Hope Theatre, Bankside on 31 October, 1614, governing the presentation and reception of the new play. Critics have scrutinized this document for evidence about how Jonson really wanted his plays to be watched; but what that kind of reading rather solemnly ignores is that the scene is a spoof, a piece of parody–legal clowning (anticipating the playful handling of several legal documents in the course of the action proper) which acknowledges that the relationship between the show and the audience can't really be bound by formal agreements, and at the same time invites the audience to play at being parties to such a contract. (It has, itself, one or two carnival traces: the public have put their seals to it 'preposterously' – i.e., in the wrong order, having paid their money when they came into the theatre – and are now invited to add their hands, a pun which converts the juridical mark of a signature into the collective and festive one of applause.) The act of coming to see the play is retextualized as participation in a game. The carnivalizing assertion of the audience within the play is matched by a special gesture extended to the audience of it.

This textual openness to the presence of the literal audience is peculiar to *Bartholomew Fair*, and contrasts especially strongly with the uncompromising authorialism of Jonson's previous play, *Catiline*. What made it possible in this one case? One answer, ironically, is that its formal source is the court masque. In that genre, which Jonson had been developing for a decade, the fictions of the text are grounded in the definite circumstances of a single performance. In that genre too, the dramatic texture is open in the sense that the text isn't supposed to be self-completing, but reaches out for its completion to the real presence in which it is performed. What Jonson has done, then, is to adapt the strategies of court entertainment for the popular stage. Instead of Whitehall, the Hope, a grubby open stage which doubled as a bear-baiting arena. Instead of the ordering gaze of the royal spectator, the heteroglot audience, conferring on the play its very different kinds of order. Instead of Elysian bowers, fairground booths. Instead of the scenic miracles of Inigo Jones, the puppets and hobby-horses of Lantern Leatherhead. The inversions – emphasized by the unusual arrangement whereby the play was performed at the Hope and at court on successive days – are quite simple; moreover, they're authorized by the masque itself, which, as we saw, cultivated just this kind of symmetrical negation of its meanings in the convention of anti-masque. By removing this upside-down comic form from its proper place in the iconography of absolutism and staging it in the public theatre, Jonson arrives at an uncrowned celebration, a masque for the people.

5   Conclusion

Things deprived suddenly of their putative meaning, the place assigned them in the ostensible order of things … make us laugh. Initially, therefore, laughter is the province of the Devil. It has a certain malice to it (things have turned out differently from the way they tried to seem), but a certain beneficent relief as well (things are looser than they seemed, we have greater latitude in living with them, their gravity does not oppress us).[1]

I've taken *Bartholomew Fair* to be a somewhat idyllic moment in Jonson's troubled relationship with his audience, and it's not quite possible to leave it at that. The parody–legal contract of the Induction is also parody–commercial: it states what theatrical goods the author is undertaking to deliver, and upon what conditions of sale. It's a game, certainly, but not an altogether good-natured one:

It is further agreed that every person here, have his or their freewill of censure, to like or dislike at their own charge, the Author having now departed with his right: it shall be lawful for any man to judge his six pennorth, his twelve pennorth, so to his eighteen pence, two shillings, half a crown, to the value of his place: Provided always his place get not above his wit. And if he pay for half a dozen, he may censure for all them too, so he will undertake that they shall be silent. He shall put in for censures here, as they do for lots at the lottery: marry, if he drop but sixpence at the door, and will censure a crown's worth, it is thought there is no conscience, or justice in that. (Induction, 75–85)

Who is to judge a play? In the classical framework, it was the wise man as opposed to the 'noise of opinion, from whose crude and airy reports I appeal, to that great and singular faculty of judgment in your Lordship, able to vindicate truth from error' (*Catiline*, Dedication, 5–8). That's the authoritarian opposition we saw earlier: truth against error, the noble patron against the vulgar, 'singular' judgement against the inanity of the multitude. In turning away, temporarily, from that absolutist model of reception, Jonson embraces a parodically business-like one: everybody has the right to judge to the extent that he's paid for it, so that if you want your opinion to outweigh the next man's, what you do is buy more tickets. It's as if Jonson, the increasingly official Court writer, is here descending into the commercial theatre and adopting what he ironically understands to be its peculiar aesthetic system. Taste is freed from State restriction and entrusted to market forces.

A market, after all, is what Bartholomew Fair essentially was, and is in the play. A typical example of the tone is the slight disagreement about the merits of the Littlewit party. When Knockem sells them Ursula's and gets them inside, Ursula is disgusted: 'sippers, sippers o' the city, they look as they would not drink off two pennorth of bottle-ale amongst 'em (III.ii.97–8). Knockem is sure she's wrong: 'Good guests, I say right hypocrites, good gluttons. In, and set a couple o' pigs o' the board, and half a dozen of the biggest bottles afore 'em, and call Whit, I do not love to hear innocents abused: fine ambling hypocrites!' (101–4) He speaks as if Ursula has been slandering them, and he's coming with generous indignation to the defence of their character. That's so in a way, but the good the argument bears upon refers exclusively to profit: Busy is a 'good' *prospect*. The Fair's attitude to its visitors is substantially the same as Jonson's declared attitude to the spectators: their value in every sense is proportionate to the value extracted from them.

This reductive and predatory mode of operation is not independent of the festive rhythms of the comedy: there's no humanist balance sheet with popular affirmation on one side and individual exploitation on the other. For the open, inorganic connectedness of the crowd *is*, in the end, the totality of the exchanges that are made between individuals within it – Quarlous blackmails Edgeworth, Edgeworth rooks Cokes, Cokes buys up Leatherhead's stall, Leatherhead takes a shilling from Littlewit to get Busy arrested, and so on. This system of transactions, generating the play's network of indirect, non-hierarchical relationships, and producing each of the *dramatis personae* in several different roles, is the main condition for the carnival plurality of the dramatic subject. The appropriate setting for the St Bartholomew games of reversal and uncrowning is the market place – not because it's picturesque, but exactly because it contains a market, a structure of relationships which at once individuates and universalizes the subjects that operate it.

One notable effect of this dynamic is the dissolution of family ties. Mrs Overdo and Mrs Littlewit are detached from their husbands and all but launched on the market as whores; Win, Cokes and Grace all escape from the authority of their 'governors'; Purecraft abandons her maternal role to embark on a career of 'madness'. It's consistent with this that, as I mentioned earlier, the Fair itself is an association of autonomous individuals; Ursula's extended 'family' of business connections has nothing to do with kinship. A parallel unpicking and rearranging of relationship is central to the structure of *Volpone*: Corvino betrays his wife, Lady Politic her husband, and Corbaccio his son, as they all take their places as clients in Volpone's system of exploitation. By the end, when Mosca joins in too, and is actively consdiered as a son-in-law by one

of the judges, the competition for the legacy has, in a famous
formulation,

> pitilessly torn asunder the motley feudal ties that bound
> man to his 'natural superiors', and has left remaining
> no other nexus betwen man and man than naked self-
> interest, than callous 'cash payment' ... has torn away
> from the family its sentimental veil, and has reduced the
> family to a mere money relation.[2]

It's a moral outrage, of course. But what the concentrated
irony of Marx and Engels in that passage adds is that it's a
liberation of energy which leaves the moralism flat-footed and
laughable. In the high parodic art of Volpone and Mosca,
and the wan piety, always close to the absurd, of Celia
and Bonario, the same dialectical laughter shakes the ethical
rigidities of Jonson's satire.

Money is the element of Volpone's imagery of transformations:

> See, here, a rope of pearl; and each, more orient
> Than that the brave Egyptian queen caroused:
> Dissolve, and drink 'em. See, a carbuncle,
> May put out both the eyes of our St Mark;
> A diamond would have bought Lollia Paulina,
> When she came in, like star-light, hid with jewels
> That were the spoils of provinces; take these,
> And wear, and lose 'em: yet remains an ear-ring
> To purchase them again....
>
> (III.vii.190–8)

Lollia Paulina's jewels represent pillaged territories; the diamond Volpone holds represents her jewels; the ear-ring represents the diamond and more. The orgiastic rhythm of
taking, losing, taking again dissolves each item on the glit-
tering list into the next like the pearls dissolving in wine. The
medium of the metaphoric transitions is exchange value; one
object absorbs another into itself by being able to buy it; this

is literally the poetry of commodities. Matter takes on an alchemical fluidity when exposed to the disintegrating and reconstituting power of its pure, universal form: money.

The specific historical form of this socio-economic alchemy is the monetarization of landed property. Kastril's estate, Face explains to him, will soon be gone:

As men of spirit hate to keep earth long.
(*Alchemist*, III.iv.84)

It's a reverberant double pun. The social sense is that the gallants Kastril wants to emulate soon turn their land into cash to support an urban lifestyle of gambling and conspicuous consumption. This process is impudently dignified by the alchemical sense, which is that there's an immanent repulsion, a chemical hatred, between earth as the grossest element and spirit as the most refined. Land, on this analogy, is the base metal in the economic alembic, trapping the spirit of wealth within the cumbersome bodies of soil, buildings, animals and customary constraints. Money, with its volatile capacity for transference, its endless convertibility, is wealth in its exalted form: purged of the corporeal contaminations of use, it circulates as pure exchange value. In another pregnant equivoque, the name for this spiritualization of wealth is 'projection', which in the economic sphere means the speculative investment of capital, but in alchemy means the exposure of inferior substances to the transmuting influence of the Stone. Projection springs money from its fixation on land and puts it through a kaleidoscopic succession of embodiments: as another projector, Merecraft, says:

Via pecunia! When she's run and gone,
And fled and dead; then will I fetch her again
With aqua-vitae, out of an old hogshead!
While there are lees of wine, or dregs of beer,
I'll never want her! Coin her out of cobwebs,
Dust, but I'll have her! Raise wool upon eggshells,

Sir, and make grass grow out o' marrow-bones,
To make her come.

(*The Devil Is An Ass*, II.i.3–10)

Some of these ingredients are from the folklore of alchemy, and the list as a whole is a crescendo of unnaturalness. Like alchemy, financial speculation breaks with the necessities of nature which confine agrarian capital, and subjects matter to the perfecting violence of art.

The enactment of this violence, in the story of the country squire who comes to London and is expropriated by lawyers, financiers and swindlers, recurs so obsessively in Jonson and his contemporaries as to give the impression that the plays document an aggressive social revolution, with the landed gentry crumbling under the pressure of mercantile and finance capital. This is misleading: although there were no doubt individual country squires who fell into debt and dispossesion through bad luck or bad judgement, the wealth and power of the rural gentry as a class were on the increase; and although it was newly possible to make large fortunes in the City, merchant capitalism was not yet the decisive economic force it was to become after (and partly through) the Revolution.[3] The historical content of the figure of Sogliardo, Kastril, Cokes, Fitzdottrel and the rest is of a different kind: it encodes the *ideological* incapacity of a customary social formation founded on self-sufficiency, hospitality, and 'natural' authority, confronted by the flexible individualism of the metropolitan (and metropolitanizing) market. Face's parenthetic remark about earth and spirit prefaces his description of a magical glass which he says Subtle can provide. By looking into its different facets, one can gain simultaneous access to the three separate components of a complicated market in credit and commodities: the device is effectively a real time business information system (III.iv.87–99). The conflict of timescales is extreme: on the one hand, the heir, constituted as an economic subject by the secular rhythms of growth and inheritance; and on the other, the projector, whose pursuit of instant profit from the movements of prices and discounting rates leads him to construct a prismatic time of non-relational simultaneities rather like the one which, as we saw, governs the dramatic construction of *Bartholomew Fair*.

Within that opposition, Jonson is authorially committed to the conservative values of organicism and authority. The fatuity of the heritors doesn't mean that their expropriation can be presented as positive; the projector is always parasitic on some more 'natural' mode of accumulation. Even in the relatively permissive atmosphere of *Bartholomew Fair*, it's made very clear that all the significant Fair people are criminals, and that the law enforcement is not only ineffective, arresting all the wrong people, but also has close business links with the crooks (III.i.1–7). The spiritualization of wealth is a satiric image of monetarization, implying that profit divorced from natural increase is a kind of *deceptio visus*, either a fantasy itself or the disreputable proceeds of manipulating the fantasies of others. The adventures of the released spirit may be alluring, even liberating, but never natural or authentic – in other words, there isn't even the most provisional articulation of a bourgeois ideology.

But then just that absence is a rather conspicuous one. After all, if the comic playwright himself were to be assigned to one or other of the opposed temporal modes, it would be to that of contemporaneity and exchange. Urban, landless and masterless, producing fictions for a fashion-conscious and uncertainly profitable market, he is the type of that hand-to-mouth entrepreneurialism which Kastril calls 'living by the wits'. Conversely, Mosca and Face, as we've seen, are monsters of deception but also artists, parodists, architects of situation, carnivalesque satirists. The comic author enters his text in criminal form.

Thus to the transgressive images· of theatre – alchemy, sexuality, plague, carnival – which play across Jonson's dramatic writing and fissure its ideological coherence, we can add that of capitalism. It's *written* as a demonic image, a negation of nature, good sense and legitimacy; but at the same time it's one with which the *writing* – as stage action, textual productivity – is deeply complicit. This contradiction, it should be clear, is not the compromised expression of anybody's subjective ambivalence about the monetarization of social relations in Jacobean London. It's not a question of balance: capitalism, as an insidious attack on the solidity and integrity of people and things, is *wholly* evil; and the theatre, as another, is *wholly* complicit with it. Consequently, a vital aspect of the text – the dimension of linguistic *play* (in every sense) without which structured communication is inconceivable – is closed to the moral intentions of the author. It's this impediment to his moralism that prevents Jonson from actually achieving the 'natural' closures of language and character which his explicit aesthetic programme designates as proper to drama. Unaccommodated by any ideology which could humanize its demonic polysemy, money permeates the plays, dislocating relationships, overturning authority, detaching signs from referents and values from things, disorganizing the world. To say this, though, is not simply to dismiss authorial intention with a gesture of textual libertarianism. The euphoric spectacle of misrule is produced as much by the moralism as by the theatrical dynamic which blocks it: it's easy to think of later workings of the theme – Restoration comedies, for example – where the ideological complicity of the theatre is accepted with a much more assured cynicism, but where, exactly for that reason, the social existence of money has become invisible.

For Jonson was writing in the gap described by R.H. Tawney, when traditional, essentially medieval, economic morality had failed to cope with the energy and intelligence of rising capitalism, but had not yet been superseded by a 'Political Arithmetic' which would separate economics and ethics altogether. Of the decay of the traditional social doctrine Tawney comments: 'When mankind is faced with the choice between exhilirating activity and piety imprisoned in a mass of desiccated formulae, it will choose the former, though the energy be brutal and the intelligence narrow.'[4] In

Tawney's narrative this observation has an elegiac note: the all-too-human penchant for action is acknowledged with tolerant regret in the consciousness that it will end in tears. Jonson produces *both* sides of just this dilemma with less tolerance and less regret. Overdo, the pious prisoner of desiccated formulae, is a pompous buffoon whose paternalist pretensions are joyfully and heartlessly torn to pieces; and to speak of Volpone's brutal energy and narrow intelligence would be euphemistic – he's a libidinal monster, a cunning moron.

The reason for this dual satiric freedom is that whereas the historian's discourse seeks to enclose the opposing tendencies within the unitary consciousness of an expository voice, the comic theatre text, exposing the issues to the dialogizing laughter of the public, can back each tendency unreservedly at different moments in the 'unresolved alterity'[5] of authorial statement and theatrical show. The conjuring trick of capital accumulation; the anarchic capacity of exchange value to transform everything into something else; the cat's-cradle of partial misunderstandings which is the market; the displacement of social and religious authority by capital's universal appeal to vanity and greed – all these harshly noted items in the conservative satirist's anatomy of abuses are capable of turning around and, as devices which substantiate and proliferate the spectacle, releasing their converse utopian potential. The comedy *about* 'projection' becomes, also, the comedy *of* projection: literally, because the performance is a speculative venture whose success, like that of Volpone's performance, is measured by the takings; but also because by turning the dangerous protean forces of the market place into games, the show raises the possibility of mastering them. These are games which our own theatre, as it seeks protection from the idiocy of the market in the liberal humanist pieties of the Arts Council, could cheer itself up by learning to play.

Notes

The place of publication is London, unless otherwise stated.

References to Jonson's works

The standard text of Jonson's works is *Ben Jonson*, edited by C. H. Herford and Percy and Evelyn Simpson, eleven volumes (Oxford, 1925–52). I have used this edition's annotations extensively, and it appears in the notes as HS. For quotations, however, I've preferred modern spelling editions, as follows:

For plays: *Complete Plays*, edited by G. A. Wilkes, 4 vols (Oxford, 1981–2).
For masques: *The Complete Masques*, edited by Stephen Orgel as part of the Yale Ben Jonson (New Haven, Conn., 1969).
For poems, *Timber: or Discoveries*, and the notes on Jonson's conversation made by William Drummond of Hawthornden: *The Complete Poems*, edited by George Parfitt (Harmondsworth, 1975).

I realize that for the plays the reader is more likely to be using one of the paperback editions, by Methuen, Arnold, New Mermaids, etc. These are good editions, but not convenient for reference because no one series is anything like complete. I hope line references match up more or less (obviously they won't do so exactly when prose scenes are involved). It's worth noting, though, that Jonson follows the continental practice of starting a new scene in the text whenever a new character comes on, unlike Shakespeare's editors, for whom a scene ends only when the stage empties. Some modern editions of Jonson conform to Shakespearean practice: thus the first act of *Volpone*, which contains five scenes in the edition I have used, only has one in the Methuen edition, edited by David Cook (1962).

Chapter 1   Speaking

1 Shakespeare, *The Tempest*, I.ii.353–62, in *Complete Works*, ed. P. Alexander (1951).

2 T. S. Eliot, 'Ben Jonson', in *Selected Essays*. 3rd edn (1951), pp. 147–60 (154).
3 John Arden, 'Ben Jonson and the plumb-line', in *To Present the Pretence* (1977), pp. 25–36 (32).
4 In M. M. Bakhtin, *The Dialogic Imagination*, tr. Caryl Emerson and Michael Holquist and ed. Michael Holquist (Austin, Texas, 1981), pp. 41–83 (41–51).
5 Bakhtin, *Dialogic Imagination*, p. 46.
6 John Milton, *Paradise Lost*, ed. Helen Darbishire (Oxford, 1952), viii, 101; ii, 270–3.
7 Charles Dickens, *Bleak House* (Harmondsworth, 1971), pp. 452–3.
8 Information in this paragraph from Margot Heinemann, *Puritanism and Theatre: Thomas Middleton and Opposition Drama under the Early Stuarts* (Cambridge, 1980), pp. 1–17; and A. J. Cook, *The Privileged Playgoers of Shakespeare's London 1576–1642* (Princeton, NJ, 1981), chapters 3 and 5.
9 Quoted in E. K. Chambers, *The Elizabethan Stage*, corrected edition (4 vols, Oxford, 1951), vol. iv, p. 316. And see M. C. Bradbrook, *The Rise of the Common Player*, new edition (Cambridge, 1979), pp. 96–118.
10 This term is a coinage by Bakhtin, or rather by his translators, who also translate the same original as 'diversity of speech types'. Heteroglossia is the effective form of the principle that words signify only in particular socio-political contexts. It could be summarized as that dimension of language which systematic linguistics is obliged to suppress. See *Dialogic Imagination*, pp. 263 and 428.
11 J. Cocke, 'A common Player', prose character printed in Chambers, *Elizabethan Stage*, iv, 255–6. Other information in this paragraph from Glynne Wickham, *Early English Stages* (3 vols, 1959–81), vol. ii, part 1: *1576–1660* (1963), pp. 90–6; and J. Leeds Barroll, 'The social and literary context', in *The Revels History of Drama in English*, vol. iii: *1576–1613* (1975), pp. 1–94.
12 Information in this paragraph from G. E. Bentley, *The Profession of Dramatist in Shakespeare's Time 1590–1642* (Princeton, NJ, 1971), especially chapters 4 and 5. More recently, the mode of production of Elizabethan theatre has been discussed, in Marxist terms, in Walter Cohen, *Drama of a Nation: Public Theater in Renaissance England and Spain* (Ithaca, NY, 1985), pp. 162–85. Cohen argues convincingly that the structure of the acting companies was artisanal rather than capitalistic, and that the real capitalists in the case were the owners of the theatre *buildings*. This, however, doesn't alter either the capitalist character of the *relationship* between companies and writers, or the fact that a place in the auditorium was a commodity. Cohen's conclusion – that in England and Spain the theatre was marked by 'the subversion of aristocratic and clerical superstructures by artisanal substructure' – is broadly in line with my own suggestion about the public theatre's dialogization of the Court word.
13 'Conversations with William Drummond', line 586.
14 HS, i, 84.
15 See L. L. Peck, 'Court patronage and government policy: the Jacobean dilemma', in *Patronage in the Renaissance*, ed. G. F. Lytle and S. Orgel (Princeton, NJ, 1981), pp. 27–46.
16 *Ars Poetica*, line 25. Jonson translates, 'Myself for shortness labour, and I grow / Obscure.'

17 Phrase from *Epigrams* LXV, 'To My Muse'.
18 See Bentley, *The Profession of Dramatist*, pp. 282–3.
19 See J. A. Barish, 'Jonson and the loathèd stage', in *A Celebration of Ben Jonson*, ed. W. Blisset et al. (Toronto, 1973), pp. 27–53.
20 The edition, and some contemporary reactions to its title, are described fully in HS, ix, 13–84.
21 'I do not labour so that the crowd will admire me: I am content with a few readers.'
22 See, for example, the Inductions to *Every Man Out of his Humour*, lines 173–84, and to *Bartholomew Fair*, lines 86–93.
23 The expression is from Jean-Paul Sartre, *What Is Literature?*, tr. B. Frechtman, paperback edition (1967), pp. 60ff. My use of it here is a sceptical one.
24 'Overdetermination', a term imported into ideological analysis by Louis Althusser from the psychoanalytic theory of dreams, indicates a process whereby several ideological and socioeconomic events come to be represented in a single ideological image, which therefore both reflects and represses their diversity.
25 A point made by J. F. Danby, *Poets on Fortune's Hill* (1952), chapter 1.
26 See 'Ode to Himself' (written on the failure of *The New Inn*), especially lines 51–60.
27 Cp. L. C. Knights, *Drama and Society in the Age of Jonson* (1937), pp. 324–32.
28 Biographical details from 'Life of Ben Jonson', in HS, i, 1–118.
29 For near-contemporary material, see HS i, 113n. and 178–89, and xi, 361 and 419–20. For the myth, the most eloquent indicator is that Jonson is the only member of the English literary pantheon who is regularly referred to by his Christian name. The characteristic tone can be heard in, for instance, Coleridge (*Coleridge on the Seventeenth Century*, ed. R. F. Brinkley, reprint (NY, 1968), pp. 642–9); Carlyle (quoted in HS xi, 566–8); and Herford and Simpson themselves, who like to describe Jonson as 'doughty'. A subtler version of the same snobbery mars John Arden's essay (see note 3, above), which develops a fancifully *ouvrieriste* parallel between dramatic construction and bricklaying.
30 Bakhtin, *Dialogic Imagination*, p. 277.
31 Bakhtin, *Dialogic Imagination*, p. 325.
32 *Verfremdung*: 'making strange' – a mode of theatrical representation which is designed to make its object recognizable and unfamiliar at the same time. For acting, its basic requirement (there are others) is that neither the actor nor the spectator should identify with the person represented. 'Even if the actor plays a man possessed he must not seem to be possessed himself, for how is the spectator to discover what possessed him if he does?' *Brecht on Theatre*, ed. John Willett (1964), p. 193.
33 Literarization: 'punctuating "representation" with "formulation"' – naming the events as well as imitating them. See *Brecht on Theatre*, pp. 43–6.

Chapter 2   Characters

1 Thus, *pre*-censorship is usually, for practical reasons, carried out on scripts rather than performances: this tends to encourage the dominance of the

writer–reader line because it requires the written text to be an adequate basis for judging the acceptability of the ensuing show.

2 See Allardyce Nicoll, *The Garrick Stage* (Manchester, 1980), pp. 93–5, 117–20, 133–7, 161–72.

3 See Michael R. Booth, 'Spectacle as production style on the Victorian stage', *Theatre Quarterly*, viii, 32 (1979), pp. 8–20.

4 E.g., *Twelfth Night*, I.ii.51.

5 The texts by Dryden, Congreve and Dennis are collected in HS xi, 513–26, 554–9. For Johnson, see, e.g., the discussion of characters in the Preface, and the General Observation on *Henry IV*. *Selected Writings*, ed. Patrick Cruttwell (Harmondsworth, 1968), pp. 263–6, 292–3.

6 See *Shakespeare: The Critical Heritage*, vol. vi, ed. Brian Vickers (1981), especially extracts from William Richardson (1774, 1779, 1798), Elizabeth Griffith (1775), Maurice Morgann (1777), Thomas Whately (1785).

7 The representative English texts are Edward Young, *Conjectures on Original Composition* (1759), and William Duff, *Essay on Original Genius* (1767).

8 Information from 'The stage history of the plays', in HS ix, 163–266, and R. G. Noyes, *Ben Jonson on the English Stage 1660–1776*, reprint (NY, 1966).

9 The date of this prologue is unclear: it was probably not written for the first performance of the play's first version in 1598, and could have been added at any time before its appearance in print in 1616. Its definition of the relationship between *Every Man In* and the *Elizabethan* theatre is thus likely to be a retrospective one. See HS i, 333–5 and ix, 343–4.

10 For a clear summary of the general principles of neo-classicism in its English and literary form, see *Neo-Classical Criticism*, ed. I. Simon (1971), pp. 9–35 and the extracts which follow.

11 The unity of dramatic consciousness in the classical theatre is illuminatingly discussed in Louis Althusser, 'The "Piccolo Theatre": Bertolazzi and Brecht: notes on a materialist theatre', in *For Marx*, tr. Ben Brewster (1969), pp. 129–51 (143–51).

12 *Shakespeare: The Critical Heritage*, vi, 139.

13 For example, *Sejanus*, 'To the Readers', lines 5–21; *Volpone*, Dedication, lines 101–14.

14 Glynne Wickham, *Early English Stages*, vol. iii: *Plays and their Makers to 1576* (1981), pp. 65–82.

15 Wickham, *Early English Stages*, iii, 74–5, 120–1.

16 M. M. Bakhtin, *Rabelais and His World*, tr. H. Iswolsky (Cambridge, Mass., 1968), p. 29.

17 Robert Burton, *The Anatomy of Melancholy*, 3 vols (1948), i, 152.

18 For the context of this, see Lawrence Stone, *The Crisis of the Aristocracy*, abridged edition (Oxford, 1967), pp. 264–7.

19 See Benjamin Boyce, *The Theophrastan Character in England to 1642* (1967), pp. 11–52.

20 *Theophrastus, The Characters, and Menander, Plays and Fragments*, tr. and ed. P. Vellacott, second edition (Harmondsworth, 1973), p. 41.

21 John Earle, *Microcosmography*, ed. H. Osborne (n.d.), p. 14. This particular character first appeared in 1629. The teasingly compressed last clause means that the modest man is even less ashamed to admit having learned from another (however weak) than he is to learn. The cultivation of extreme

conciseness was a deliberate stylistic grace of the genre, associated, I think, with the metaphor of charactery as inscription.

22 Stone, *Crisis of the Aristocracy*, pp. 303–7.

23 W. J. Ong, *Rhetoric, Romance and Technology* (1971), p. 56.

24 See the title story in Franz Kafka, *In the Penal Settlement*, tr. E. Kaiser and E. Wilkins (1949).

25 HS iii, 602–3.

26 See Wickham, *Early English Stages*, ii, 1, 267–75.

27 Stephen Orgel, 'The royal theatre and the role of king', in *Patronage in the Renaissance*, ed. Lytle and Orgel, pp. 261–73.

28 For a virtuoso discussion of the optical relations of this picture, see Michel Foucault, *The Order of. Things*, English edition (1970), pp. 3–16.

29 The exact dispositions of the Elizabethan playhouses are the subject of a long-running scholarly debate. The details which are agreed upon are conveniently summarized in R. Watkins and J. Lemmon, *In Shakespeare's Playhouse: The Poet's Method* (Newton Abbott, 1974), pp. 22–31. This book is the introduction to a series on individual plays; each volume contains a brief recapitulation of the original account.

30 Not an accidental analogy: see Wickham, *Early English Stages*, ii, 2, 30–62 for an account of the semantic and functional overlap between 'game-houses' and 'playhouses'. The games in question – bull and bear baiting, cockfighting and jousting – were violently competitive and often accompanied by gambling; that is, they were spectacles in which the focus of attention split and shifted rapidly and unpredictably. The formal similarity to Jonson's articulation of stage groupings, by advantage, conspiracy, depredation and competition, is striking.

31 Aristotle, *On the Art of Poetry*, chapter 5 in *Classical Literary Criticism*, tr. and ed. T. S. Dorsch (Harmondsworth, 1965), p. 37.

32 Sir Philip Sidney, *An Apology for Poetry*, ed. G. Shepherd (1965), p. 136.

33 Sidney, *Apology for Poetry*, pp. 117, 137.

34 Chambers, *Elizabethan Stage*, iv, 224.

35 For example, *Volpone*, Prologue, lines 33–6.

36 See *Volpone: A Casebook*, ed. J. A. Barish (1972), pp. 29–30, 41.

37 Misrule: the festive state of affairs, associated with Christmas and carnival time, when control passes from the legitimate governor to a topsy-turvy official whose function is to keep good order and normality at bay. See Enid Welsford, *The Fool* (1935), pp. 197–217.

38 Lawrence Stone, *The Causes of the English Revolution 1529–1642* (1972), p. 85.

39 See Stone, *Crisis of the Aristocracy*, pp. 191–207; and Christopher Hill, *Reformation to Industrial Revolution* (Harmondsworth, 1969), pp. 67–8, 94–7. 101–8.

40 Cp. Perry Anderson, *Lineages of the Absolutist State* (1974), pp. 137–41.

41 The 'bodily lower stratum' and the 'banquet for all the world' are both themes running right through *Rabelais and His World*. They are discussed together, for example, in chapter 5, pp. 303–67. See also the Introduction, pp. 18–19.

Chapter 3 Languages

1 Roland Barthes, *Camera Lucida*, translated by Richard Howard, paperback edition (1984), p. 85.

2 Bakhtin, *Dialogic Imagination*, p. 272.
3 Bakhtin, *Dialogic Imagination*, p. 273.
4 Wickham, *Early English Stages*, vol. iii, 207–9.
5 The phrase is from *Bartholomew Fair*, Induction, line 122. See also the Dedication to the *Epigrams*, lines 22–7. For Jonson's brushes with the censorship, see HS, i, 15–16, 36–9, 100.
6 *Sejanus*, I, 375–439.
7 Barthes, *Camera Lucida*, p. 80.
8 V. N. Vološinov, *Marxism and the Philosophy of Language*, translated by Ladislav Matejka and I. R. Titunik (New York, 1973), p. 72. It seems possible that much of this book was actually written by Bakhtin, and certainly Vološinov was his closest follower and collaborator. In referring to the various texts involved I've accepted all title pages at face value, while interpreting the ideas on the basis that Bakhtin–Vološinov is a single theoretician.
9 Vološinov, *Marxism and the Philosophy of Language*, p. 71.
10 Vološinov, *Marxism and the Philosophy of Language*, p. 75.
11 Bakhtin, *Dialogic Imagination*, p. 80.
12 See W. J. Ong, 'Latin language study as a Renaissance puberty rite', in *Rhetoric, Romance and Technology* (1971), pp. 113–41.
13 See *Cicero*, Loeb Classical Library, 28 vols, vol. x (1977), pp. 32–66.
14 Vološinov, *Marxism and the Philosophy of Language*, p. 80.
15 B. N. De Luna, *Jonson's Popish Plot: A Study of 'Catiline' in its Historical Context* (Oxford, 1967).
16 See Stone, *Crisis of the Aristocracy*, pp. 129–34, 303–17, 332–44.
17 Some of the pamphlets are conveniently reprinted in *Cony-Catchers and Bawdy Baskets*, edited by Gamini Salgado (Harmondsworth, 1972). For the world upside down, see Peter Burke, *Popular Culture in Early Modern Europe* (1978), plate 17.
18 In *For the Honour of Wales*, *The Irish Masque at Court*, *The Masque of Queens*, *Mercury Vindicated from the Alchemists at Court*, and *Pleasure Reconciled to Virtue*, respectively.
19 See Peter Dixon, *Rhetoric*, Critical Idiom Series, 19 (1971), pp. 26–8.
20 See L. A. Beaurline, *Jonson and Elizabethan Comedy* (1978), pp. 218–23.
21 This contradiction is outlined in a broader context in Terry Eagleton, *Walter Benjamin, or, Towards a Revolutionary Criticism* (1981), pp. 101–6.
22 Quoted in HS xi, 565.
23 There is a later activation of the same formula in Gogol's *The Government Inspector*, strikingly – though presumably coincidentally – a Jonsonian comedy.

Chapter 4 Theatre

1 See Richard Southern, *The Seven Ages of the Theatre*, paperback edition (1968), p. 70.
2 Michael Foucault, *The Order of Things*, English edition (1970), especially pp. 46–67. For a concentrated and sympathetic account of Jonson's adherence to an early (classical-Baconian) version of 'Enlightenment ideology', see

Don E. Wayne, *Penshurst: the Semiotics of Place and the Poetics of History* (1984), pp. 147–50.

3 Denis Diderot, *Le neveu de Rameau*, Livre de Poche (Paris, 1966), p. 169.

4 The name for the device whereby the objects represented within a text include the form of the text as a whole; for example, a jar with a label depicting the labelled jar.

5 The notablé exceptions are the 'problem plays', in which the Duke of Vienna's disguise, and Parolles' blindfold, are both forcibly removed in mid-scene. The attendant disenchantment is perhaps one of the things which make the plays problematic.

6 John Webster (?), 'An Excellent Actor', reprinted in Chambers, *Elizabethan Stage*, iv, 257. This phrase is almost the guiding text for B. L. Joseph, *Elizabethan Acting*, second edition (Oxford, 1964), which sets out the case for regarding Elizabethan acting as a branch of oratory.

7 Diderot, *Le neveu de Rameau*, p. 192.

8 Diderot, *Le neveu de Rameau*, p. 189.

9 John Earle, *Microcosmography*, ed. H. Osborne (n.d.), p. 57.

10 Diderot, *Le neveu de Rameau*, p. 192.

11 Bakhtin, *Rabelais and His World*, p. 433.

12 Jean Genet, *The Balcony*, tr. Bernard Frechtman, revised edition (1966).

13 Ananias is given one hour to fetch an Elder at II.v.84 and is told on his return at III.ii.1–2 that he has just made it. Face goes out at II.vi.94 to keep an appointment with Surly for which he is already late, and returns, after an impatient wait for him, at III.iii.1.

14 1610 is fixed both by the widow (II.vi.31 and IV.iv.29–30) and by Ananias (V.v.102), who also indirectly specifies the date at III.ii.130.

15 The information is from HS ix 223–4, though the editors don't draw my conclusion from it.

16 W. J. Ong, 'Latin language study as a Renaissance puberty rite', in *Rhetoric, Romance and Technology* (1971), pp. 113–41.

17 Lawrence Stone makes a precisely similar point about 'honour' in *The Family, Sex and Marriage in England 1500–1800* (1977), pp. 503–4.

18 'He who is upright in his way of life and unstained by guilt', a very well-known Renaissance tag, from Horace, *Odes*, i, 22. Horace's poem, ironically, goes on to effect a stylish resolution of stoic and amorous idealisms. 'Integer' untranslatably combines 'upright' with 'healthful' and 'one and entire'.

19 For the information about alchemy, see Charles Nicholl, *The Chemical Theatre* (1980), pp. 25–32, 38–9, 48–9.

20 See Wickham, *Early English Stages*, iii, Chapter 8.

21 See Enid Welsford, *The Fool* (1935), pp. 200–11.

22 Peter Burke, *Popular Culture in Early Modern Europe* (1978), p. 188.

23 Bakhtin, *Rabelais*, p. 219.

24 Burke, *Popular Culture*. p. 190.

25 Eagleton, *Walter Benjamin*, p. 149.

26 Burke, *Popular Culture*, p. 190.

27 See Burke, *Popular Culture*, pp. 207–22, 270–8.

28 See Christopher Hill, *The World Turned Upside Down*, paperback edition (Harmondsworth, 1975), and especially pp. 288–93.

29 *Charivari* was a parodic and disorderly celebration of a 'wrong' marriage (e.g.

a misalliance, or one in which the husband was henpecked or cuckolded). See Inga-Stina Ekeblad, 'The "Impure Art" of John Webster', reprinted in *John Webster*, ed. G. K. and S. K. Hunter, Penguin Critical Anthology (Harmondsworth, 1969), pp. 202–21 (213ff.). The ritual is also central to the form of *Epicoene*, as Ian Donaldson points out in *The World Upside-Down* (1970), pp. 39–45.

30 Antonin Artaud, *The Theater and Its Double*, tr. Mary Caroline Richards (New York, 1958), p. 118.

31 Artaud, 'The theater and the plague', in *The Theater and Its Double*, pp. 15–32.

32 Artaud, *The Theater and Its Double*, p. 24.

33 Quoted in F. P. Wilson, *The Plague in Shakespeare's London* (Oxford, 1927), p. 52.

34 Stephen Gosson, *Plays Confuted in Five Actions* (1582), quoted in Chambers, *Elizabethan Stage*, iv, 219.

35 Wilson, *The Plague in Shakespeare's London*, pp. 153–4.

36 Bakhtin, *Rabelais*, p. 187.

37 Artaud, *The Theater and Its Double*, p. 28.

38 Wolfit's enthusiasm for it at a time when Jonson was performed rarely is the most eloquent instance. Since then, it's been played by Ralph Richardson, Leo McKern, Colin Blakely and Paul Scofield, among others – a heavyweight attention which no other Jonson role has commanded since the eighteenth century. See Arnold P. Hinchcliffe, *Volpone (Text and Performance)* (1985).

39 From a note in the Revels Accounts of spending on canvas: see Chambers, *Elizabethan Stage*, iv, 183.

40 See Wickham, *Early English Stages*, i, 175–6.

41 HS, ix 245.

Chapter 5 Conclusion

1 Milan Kundera, *The Book of Laughter and Forgetting*, tr. Michael Henry Heim, paperback edition (Harmondsworth, 1983), p. 61.

2 Karl Marx and Friedrich Engels, *The Communist Manifesto*, Penguin edition (Harmondsworth, 1967), p. 82.

3 See Lawrence Stone, *The Causes of the English Revolution 1529–1642* (1972), pp. 73–6.

4 R. H. Tawney, *Religion and the Rise of Capitalism*, paperback edition (Harmondsworth, 1938), p. 189.

5 The phrase is from Louis Althusser, *For Marx*, tr. Ben Brewster (1969), p. 142.

Index